SALT *and* LIGHT

THE SECRET TO RESTORING AMERICA'S CULTURE

DANIEL J. PILLA

FOREWORD BY GARY KEESEE

Cover design by: Yvonne Parks, BOOKRALLY
Contents design by: Allan Nygren, Mosaic Productions

My special thanks to Scott MacPherson for his keen editorial eye, and the team at Printopya for their fine proofreading prowess.

Scripture quotations taken from The Holy Bible, New International Version,* NIV.* Tyndale House Publishers and Zondervan. Copyright © 1973, 1978, 1984, 2011 by Biblica, Inc.™ All rights reserved worldwide. www.zondervan.com.

Printed in the United States of America
First edition: April 2018
ISBN: 978-1-884367-11-3

NewType Publishing
www.newtypepublishing.com

Table of Contents

Is not this the kind of fasting I have chosen:
to loose the chains of injustice
and untie the cords of the yoke,
to set the oppressed free and break every yoke?
Is it not to share your food with the hungry
and to provide the poor wanderer with shelter—
when you see the naked, to clothe them,
and not to turn away from your own flesh and blood?
Then your light will break forth like the dawn,
and your healing will quickly appear;
then your righteousness will go before you,
and the glory of the LORD will be your rear guard.
Then you will call, and the LORD will answer;
you will cry for help, and he will say: Here am I.
If you do away with the yoke of oppression,
with the pointing finger and malicious talk,
and if you spend yourselves in behalf of the hungry
and satisfy the needs of the oppressed,
then your light will rise in the darkness,
and your night will become like the noonday.

Isaiah 58:6-10 (NIV)

In Loving Memory of

Tom

Foreword

To say that America is in the midst of a culture war would be an enormous understatement. The evidence can be seen in every newscast, on the cover of every newspaper, and in the very lifestyles of her citizens. I believe that just about everyone would agree that America is changing fast, and that she is not the same America she once was.

But is she changing for the better? Many believe she is going in the wrong direction, especially spiritually.

In dealing with this conflict, the finger of blame is pointed in various directions, depending on who is pointing the finger. Blame is often focused on government ("too much" or "not enough"), the economy ("too much control" or "not enough freedom"), and our public schools ("schools are deteriorating" or "kids need to spend more time there"). For solutions, we often clamor for government to spend more money on social issues. But a lack of money is not the reason that a solution to the spiritual decline in our country eludes us. Untold billions of dollars have been spent to find answers to vexing social problems, all with little or no apparent meaningful impact.

Can America be saved? Is it too late? There are many books available that advertise possible solutions, yet the problems persist and even grow worse.

In his latest book, *Salt and Light*, Dan Pilla takes a completely different approach to dealing with today's social and economic problems, one you probably will not hear on CNN or see on the display rack at your local book store. In *Salt and Light*, Dan lays out a surprisingly simple formula for dealing with America's spiritual crisis. Even better, the formula has been proven over generations to successfully lead people to prosperity and to bring peace to the land.

I know you will ask, "If the answer is that easy, and if it has a long history of a proven track record, why is it not discussed among America's elite?" That's the billion-dollar question, and Dan lays out the answer in shocking clarity, along with the formula for carrying the solution into practice.

Having spent his entire adult life battling the IRS as a tax litigator, Dan understands how to uncover hidden clues and present detailed facts that lead to favorable resolutions in very complex tax collection cases. He brings that skill and experience to bear in dealing with what is perhaps America's greatest challenge ever: her future spiritual condition. In his typical methodical, building-block approach to presenting evidence and advancing arguments, Dan lays out who the guilty party is and exactly what we can do to reverse the dangerous path we are on.

Between the fascinating historical details and the moving personal stories Dan uses to build his case, once I started reading *Salt and Light*, I just could not put this book down. It is a must-read for all of America!

Gary Keesee
Pastor, Faith Life Church, Columbus, OH
Author and host of *Fixing the Money Thing*
CEO and founder, Forward Financial Group Inc.

CHAPTER 1

Sudden Death

Imagine that you're standing at a street corner about to cross. You are with a friend and the two of you are chatting while waiting for the light to change. The light soon turns green and you both step off the curb into the street.

Your friend was looking to his right at you as he stepped off the curb to cross. Because of that, he did not see the car coming straight at him, from his blind spot on his left side. But you see the car because you are looking exactly in that direction.

As the car is barreling toward your unwary friend, you have a decision to make. What do you do? Do you alert your friend—"Watch out!" Do you grab his shoulder and pull him back? Or do you do nothing but hope he sees the car in time to get out of the way?

I rather expect that not a single person reading this thinks he would do nothing. Each of us thinks he would do something to stop a friend from walking right into the path of an oncoming car that he did not and could not see.

That scenario reminds me of my friend Tom. Tom and I worked together from 1979 to November 6, 2000. From 1996 to November 6, 2000, we worked side by side in the same office building in White Bear Lake that we built as partners in 1996. On November 6, 2000, the day before the presidential election between George W. Bush and Al Gore, Tom and I sat in my office chatting about the election in particular, politics in general, and the upcoming event we were both to participate in.

You see, later that week Tom and I were supposed to meet in Las Vegas for a seminar that I was conducting as part of my Tax Freedom Institute. The Tax Freedom Institute (TFI) is an association of tax professionals—attorneys, CPAs and Enrolled Agents—focused on the defense of taxpayers' rights and IRS problems resolution. Tom was a charter member of the organization that I started in 1993. Our convention in Las Vegas was an annual event that Tom attended every year since TFI's inception.

I met Tom in 1979. He was an attorney in Minneapolis at the time with a small private practice that focused on criminal defense. He worked a wide range of state criminal cases. I was a *very* young tax practitioner working on a wide range of civil IRS defense cases. At that time, I had no background or experience in criminal law, and Tom had no experience with the IRS.

I met Tom because, early in 1979, I met a man (Bob) from a small town in western Wisconsin, not far from my home in St. Paul. Bob heard about me through a tax activist group he was involved with. Bob was a tax protester. In those days, many of my cases involved working with tax protesters because my father was a tax protester. I got involved in tax litigation work in the first place because of my father's tax problems. I was successful in stopping the IRS from seizing my parents' home, and word of that success got around very quickly. I helped people from all over the area deal with a variety of tax problems.

But Bob's case was quite different. Up to that point, every case I handled was a civil case. In a civil case, the IRS just wants the money. But Bob was charged with a crime. The IRS wanted the money *and* a pound of flesh. They wanted Bob to spend time in a federal prison. Both Bob and I were in over our heads.

By that time, I was getting quite good at knowing what the IRS was supposed to do and spotting when they failed to follow their own rules—which was most of the time. As such, I could help with the dollars-and-cents part of the case. But I could not represent Bob in federal court as I was not licensed to do so. But even if I were, I knew nothing about criminal procedure and jury trials. Bob needed an experienced trial attorney, so I set out to find someone to work with us.

Through a series of referrals, I found Tom. He and I met at his office in south Minneapolis and we picked each other's brains. He learned about me and my experiences and I learned about him and his. As it turned out, we were kindred spirits. We shared the same views on limited government, free market economics (Tom's undergraduate degree was in economics), out-of-control government agencies, politics in general, and we both had an abiding respect for the Constitution.

And most important, Tom loved baseball. In fact, time would reveal to me that he was a scientist when it came to baseball. He knew the game inside and out. He understood the nuances like nobody I ever met before or since. He loved the Minnesota Twins and he had season tickets to the Twins for years. Over time, we spent many hours at Twins games, talking about baseball and what the Twins needed to do to get to the next level, as well as talking about politics, economics and the Constitution.

Tom even coached youth baseball with me for several years. When my oldest son, Anthony, was ten years old, I coached his team in a Stillwater, Minnesota, church league. Even though Tom had no kid of his own in the program, he offered to coach along with me. He did so for three years. During that time, he sacrificed his evenings at least four days a week for eleven weeks of the season, unselfishly helping twelve kids he didn't know learn to play the game the right way.

Most of those evenings, Tom had dinner at my house before our practices. My two youngest kids were about four and six years old during this time. They loved Tom. Every night that he ate dinner with us, he brought with him some stupid joke that just cracked them up. And our baseball teams were great all three years. In one season, our team was undefeated (that is, if you don't count the championship game, which we lost 5-3).

Tom and I spent an inordinate amount of time together in the first few months of our association, getting ready for Bob's trial. We spent long hours viewing the mountains of documents in the case, interviewing prospective witnesses, reviewing grand jury testimony, laying out trial strategy, and preparing Bob for the challenge of his life—testifying in his own defense in a federal criminal tax trial.

The case went to trial in Madison, Wisconsin, in the fall of 1979. Tom and I stayed in a hotel in Madison. Between the time in court and the countless after-hours tasks, we worked fourteen hours a day for a week. Unfortunately, Bob's case did not have a favorable outcome. He was convicted of willful failure to file his income tax returns as charged. Though we were disappointed, given the amount of work we invested, none of us (including Bob) was surprised, given the evidence in the case of Bob's extensive tax protester background and actions.

But my friendship with Tom was forged in the crucible of Bob's criminal prosecution. Tom and I went on, over the next twenty years, to work together on just about every kind of tax case you can imagine. We represented hundreds of clients before the IRS in audit and collection cases, and we prosecuted innumerable civil cases before the United States Tax Court. What's more, we worked on another dozen or so criminal cases, much like Bob's, in which we labored night and day in the defense of our clients.

In 1988, when the IRS decided to target me because of my high-profile attacks on the agency through my many media appearances and books (I had written three by then), Tom was at my side throughout the ordeal. Early in the process, we obtained through the Freedom of Information Act a memo that was written by the Chief of the Examination (audit) function of the IRS in St. Paul describing their plan of attack on me. It was abundantly clear from the memo that the IRS's attack had nothing whatsoever to do with whether they believed I broke the law, or even that I owed money for some innocent reason due to a good faith mistake of some kind.

Rather, it was clear that they simply didn't like what I was doing. The memo stated that "Pilla is the most sophisticated outspoken opponent of the IRS and we must discredit him in the eyes of the public." The memo went on to describe exactly how the IRS would work to bring me down in an all-out effort to stop the work I was doing to bring justice to taxpayers across the nation.

As the case progressed, it became obvious to the IRS that not only had I not broken any law but also that I didn't owe the IRS a dime in taxes; so they simply resorted to treachery. They offered a bribe (that's right, I said *bribe*) to my publisher. The offer was that he would swear to the IRS that he paid me $150,000 in royalties on which I never paid taxes, and in exchange for the lie, he would get a refund of all the taxes he had paid personally.

What do you do with that?

As we discussed strategy, Tom said, "Let's set 'em up."

"What do you mean?" I asked.

"Let's make them think we are going to take the deal. I'll get the auditor on the phone and make him believe that Dave [my publisher] wants to go for the deal. I'll ask him how it will work, what Dave has to do, and how we can be sure Dave gets the money. I'll get him to explain it all."

Dave and I looked at each other, then we asked, "Okay, then what?"

Tom said, "I'll be recording the conversation. I'll get him on tape offering the bribe and explaining just how the scam will work. Then, when the time is right, we'll release the tape."

And that's just what we did. Tom had a lengthy call with the agent, who had no idea his every word was being recorded. But Tom convinced him that Dave was taking the deal. The agent explained all the sordid details and announced that he was going forward with the paperwork to make the claim against me.

Shortly thereafter, I received a bill from the IRS for taxes, interest and confiscatory penalties well in excess of $100,000 due to the "unreported income" I allegedly received from my publisher. The bill carried appeal rights, which I promptly exercised. When the case came up for review by the IRS's attorneys in St. Paul, I appeared at the offices of the IRS's counsel—along with the tape. The attorney representing the IRS looked at the tape sitting on the conference table as he read the transcript that was prepared for him in advance. The meeting lasted only as long as it took the attorney to read the transcript. The IRS dropped all claims against me—and they have left me alone ever since.

In 1996, Tom and I built a small office building in White Bear Lake, Minnesota. We operated our businesses out of that office and rented the remainder of the space. Tom was devoted exclusively to the practice of law and I was split between tax litigation and book writing. Every single day, Tom and I strategized about tax cases, political issues, economic matters, and Twins baseball.

That's exactly what we were doing on Monday, November 6, 2000, at about three o'clock in the afternoon. I was sitting at my computer table and Tom was sitting at my desk across from me. He was about to leave to go to Phoenix, where he and his father owned a condo. He would spend a few days there with his dad and then meet me in Las Vegas on Thursday. Thursday evening would be the start of the three-day seminar I would conduct for the Tax Freedom Institute. Since Tom was a charter member of TFI's advisory board, his role at the seminar was critical.

Tom walked out of my office that afternoon and I went back to my work. I never saw him again. The next morning, I voted in the election and then, later that day, headed to Las Vegas. Late Wednesday night, I got a call from home. I was told that Tom died earlier that day, November 8, 2000, of a massive heart attack at his condo in Phoenix. He was rollerblading earlier that day and, when he arrived home, sat in a chair, closed his eyes, and never woke up. He was gone—and I was stunned. I sat in absolute silence while on the phone for I don't know how long.

The next evening my seminar began with a business meeting for all TFI members. I expected Tom to be there to help me with the meeting. Instead of inviting Tom to the front to speak as I did in each of the past seven years, I announced to the group that he was dead. He was just 53 years of age.

I miss Tom every day. I miss his wit, his intelligence, his insight into political and economic matters, his insight into the Constitution, his wise counsel, and his love of baseball. To this very day—*seventeen years after his passing*—I cannot watch or listen to a Twins baseball game without thinking of Tom.

But the thing that haunts me the most—the thing that I will take to my *grave*—is that in all the years of our friendship, in all the work we did together, in all the personal time we spent talking about corrupt politicians, unconstitutional laws, and Twins baseball, *I never once* talked with Tom about the Savior of the world, the key to everlasting life—Jesus Christ.

CHAPTER 2

Gideon's First Mission

It's not as if I knew Tom was going to have a heart attack. I didn't have a premonition of any kind. And it's not like I watched him step off the curb into oncoming traffic without warning him. I certainly would have warned him. But isn't it just as important to talk to your friends about spiritual danger as well as physical danger? In the physical sense, death ends one's life in this earthly realm. The loved one's absence is real and is dearly missed, no doubt. But spiritual death separates oneself from God *for all eternity.*

As Christians, we know it is only through the shed blood of Jesus Christ that our relationship with God is restored. Though Jesus was without sin, He voluntarily took on the sin of the world so that all humanity may have an eternal relationship with God. Without such a relationship, there can be no communion with God. So why do we—why did *I*—shy away from talking about such a critical issue to such a close friend?

The question is particularly vexing when you consider that the message is not *bad news*. It's not as if you've been tapped to tell your best friend she's dying of cancer. On the contrary, the truth about God's love and grace and His promise of everlasting life is the best of news.

So why don't we share it?

We've all heard the expression that says you never talk about religion and politics to friends and family. All it does is start a fight, create anxiety, and strain relationships. Maybe that's true. We all have an uncle or niece, brother or cousin, who's diametrically opposed to addressing any matters of faith, God or religion. Maybe they are afraid to face their own mortality. Maybe they have a profoundly guilty conscience that forces them to avoid the subject. Maybe they are just blissfully ignorant—and determined to stay that way—of the fact that they will face God upon their death and will be called to account for their actions.

Regardless, one scriptural model boldly suggests that family and friends are exactly the *first* place we should begin talking about the promise of salvation and the gift of eternal life through the shed blood of Jesus Christ. That model comes from the story of Gideon in the book of Judges, chapters 6 and 7.

We are all probably familiar with the story of Gideon's army. God chose Gideon to lead Israel from the bondage and oppression of the Midianites and Amalekites. Before Gideon faced the enemy, God winnowed his army down from 32,000 men to just 300. Those 300 men then defeated the army of the oppressors, which was so big, it is said the enemy were as thick as locusts and their camels were more numerous than the sands of the seashore (see Judges 7:12). By the time the battle was over, Gideon and his tiny band had the enemy whipped and on the run (see Judges 7:22-23).

Without question, this is an inspiring story and there is much to learn from it. But to be sure, it is just a small part of the story of Gideon's rise to leadership. In fact, Gideon's battle with the Midianites is the *third* mission that God sent him on. The story of Gideon's *first* mission is rarely told and even less understood. It is highly relevant to my assertion that family and friends are to be the starting point of our missionary work, not the ending point—and in any event, they most certainly are not to be ignored.

The history of Israel as recounted in Judges takes place over a period of about 400 years. During that time, Israel went through six successive periods of oppression. The pattern was very clear and repeated itself over and over. God's people would abandon His laws and commands. They would seek their own pleasure and do as they pleased without regard to any consequences. They would fall into long periods of idolatry and hedonism (see Judges 17:6).

Because of the sin of disobedience, the people lost God's protection. It's not like God abandoned them. On the contrary, God never turns His back on His people. Rather, the people walked away from God. They turned to idol worship and self-gratification on a grand scale. That is to say, they willfully left the sanctuary God prepared for them and found themselves on their own in a very dangerous and evil world. This is precisely the story of the prodigal son as told by Jesus in Luke chapter 15. It was the son who left his father's estate and squandered his wealth on wild living (hedonism). The father did not turn his back on the son (see Luke 15:11-16).

Having lost God's protection, the Israelites fell under the domination and oppression of foreign powers. They were oppressed severely during these periods, and when the oppression became too great to bear, they cried out to God. They begged forgiveness and returned to obeying God's commands. Owing to the repentance of the people and their reestablishment of God's rules, God raised up someone to deliver them. Such a leader, not unlike Moses, led Israel against its oppressors and restored liberty. There was peace for a time and the people prospered again. That peace and prosperity created complacency in the people's hearts and arrogance in their minds. The disobedience of God's commands started yet again. And the pattern repeated itself.

Gideon was one of those deliverers.

In the time of Gideon, Israel had been oppressed by the Midianites for seven years because Israel "did evil" in God's eyes (Judges 6:1). Judges 6:2-3 explains that the oppression of the Midianites was so great that the Israelites had to hide out in the mountains. The Midianites destroyed their crops and stole their livestock. Nothing was left for Israel after the land was ravaged (see Judges 6:4-6). But, in keeping with the pattern explained earlier, Israel cried out to God, begging for relief.

God heard their cry and sent them a prophet. A prophet, speaking for God, reminded Israel that God is the ultimate deliverer, that He brought them out of Egypt, rescuing them from slavery. He defeated their enemies. The prophet reminded them of God's simple command: "I am the Lord—do not worship other gods." The prophet also pointed out that the current oppression was their own doing because they did not listen to God (see Judges 6:7-10).

Next, God sent an angel to Gideon to tell Gideon that he was being tapped to be the deliverer of Israel. The angel addressed Gideon as a "mighty warrior." I find this fascinating since at the time of this visit, Gideon was not waging war against anybody. Quite the opposite, in fact: he was hiding (see Judges 6:12). He knew of the oppression of Israel. He saw the evil all around him. But he did nothing about it. Instead, he hid from the enemy, threshing his wheat in a winepress to keep the Midianites from stealing it.

Not only was Gideon not waging any kind of war, but also it seems that he embraced an attitude of *defeatism*. He showed no excitement at the prospect of leading Israel. His first words to the angel question why God abandoned them. He wonders how this evil could have happened if God was with them (see Judges 6:13). The answer, of course, lies back in verse 1. God didn't abandoned Israel. Israel did evil by ignoring God's commands and pursuing her own hedonism.

After a lengthy discussion and a series of signs from God, Gideon became convinced that he was the man for the job after all. Gideon built an altar to the Lord (see Judges 6:24). And that is when God gave Gideon his first assignment, well before he ever marched on the Midianite army with his ragtag band of 300 soldiers. His assignment was to purge idols.

The Israelites strayed so far from God's commands that they had taken to worshiping the false gods and idols of their oppressors. This overt and unashamed violation of God's first commandment was precisely why they were in bondage. Even Gideon's own father built an altar to Baal and erected an Asherah pole next to it (see Judges 6:25).

Baal was a mythical god believed by pagans to control the earth. Baal was believed to control the weather, the growth of vegetation, and the production of agriculture. The false god was generally depicted in the form of a bull to symbolize strength and fertility. It would have been carved from wood, stone or ivory.

Asherah was said to be the female counterpart to Baal. She was alleged to be the mother goddess of the sea. This false god was worshiped by means of a carved wooden pillar, known as an Asherah pole.

Gideon's first mission from God was very specific: he was to tear down his father's altar to Baal and cut down the Asherah pole. He was then to build a proper altar to God, and taking a bull from his father's herd, he was to make a proper sacrifice, using the wood of the Asherah pole for the fire (see Judges 6:25-26).

There are three very critical points in this portion of Gideon's story:

1. Gideon is to destroy his father's idols. These were idols erected by and used in Gideon's own family. It seems clear to me that the job of rescuing Israel from bondage and oppression started *right at home*. Gideon could not deliver Israel without first delivering his family. You can't rescue generally unless you rescue specifically.
2. Gideon must send the people the same clear message the angel gave to him: God doesn't tolerate idolatry. The ancients worshiped all manner of false gods and erected various idols in their images. While we don't often see altars to Baal or Asherah poles as used in the ancient world, there is plenty of idolatry all around us nevertheless.

    Idolatry is really nothing more than the "worship" of or holding greater loyalty to anything but the living God of Abraham, Isaac and Jacob, and His resurrected Son, Jesus. Anything you put ahead of God becomes a form of idolatry. In our society, this comes in many forms. Most certainly money is high on the list. People chase money as though it's an end in itself rather than a tool to be used for the greater good of those around them. It also shows up it the form of hobbies, possessions and toys. Some people idolize their jobs or titles. This list could go on, but you get the point.

Placing any thing or any person ahead of God in your loyalty and commitment constitutes idolatry and is a violation of the first two commandments. That's why God hates it so much. It causes sensual excesses and hedonism. It contributes to stress and confusion in relationships. And generally, it causes chaos in society at various levels. Ultimately, it leads to spiritual weakness and cultural decline. We see it all around us today, as I discuss in more detail later.

3. Gideon was to build a *proper* altar to God on the very place where his father's altar to Baal once stood. He was to burn the wood from the Asherah pole to make a *proper* sacrifice to God, as expressed in His law. That is to say, after destroying the false idols, he was to restore God to His rightful place as expressed in the first commandment.

Today, we don't sacrifice bulls or doves because Jesus was the final and ultimate sacrifice for all sin. Today's "proper altar" is the cross of Christ. The sacrifice is His shed blood, which is the only means of restoring our relationship with God and the liberty it brings.

The lessons of Gideon's story in 6:25-26 are clear to me. See if you don't agree:

1. Never mind what others say about religion and politics at home. We have to start the process of witnessing about God's salvation right at home, with those around us and closest to us.
2. We have to "tear down" the idols we see around us, but certainly not in a physical or violent sense. Rather, we must do so verbally, by

witnessing in love and kindness about sin and restoration. We have to point out idolatry where we see it.

3. Finally—and critically—we must introduce our loved ones to the love and saving grace that are offered as a free gift through the shed blood of Jesus, God's own Son, and from no other source.

CHAPTER 3

Intimidation Is Silencing the Church in America

For decades, secularists have been hard at work scrubbing America's Christian identity out of her culture. They have successfully removed prayer and Bible reading from our public schools and institutions. They have taken the Ten Commandants out of our courts and councils. They have even managed to mostly eviscerate the truth of our Christian history. They have managed to convince our young people that America was founded as a secular nation by secular people. What's worse, they have succeeded in stigmatizing Christianity through a relentless barrage of name-calling, accusing Christians of being bigoted, hate-filled, racist, homophobic, Islamaphobic, xenophobic, sexist, boorish Nazis.

It's to the point where it is now widely *and falsely* believed that America is indeed a secular nation. We are told that if you want to be a Christian, okay, but shut up and do so in private and keep your irrelevant, narrow-minded opinions to yourself.

Perhaps that's why we too often keep our mouths shut when it comes to witnessing about the gospel. Is the blizzard of name-calling and intimidation at the hands of secularists silencing the church in America? To the extent that intimidation is a key factor, it is successful only because too many Christians are ignorant of America's Christian history. To push back against this barrage of intimidation against the church, American Christians need to know the truth about our history.

The truth is, it wasn't that long ago that Christianity prevailed—by far and away—as the most pervasive religion in America. In fact, as late as 1892, in the case of *Holy Trinity Church v. United States*, 143 U.S. 457, 464 (1892), the Supreme Court of the United States, believe it or not, overtly and conspicuously confirmed this fact.

The *Holy Trinity Church* case grew from a New York church that found itself in trouble with the U.S. government over alleged immigration law violations. The church brought a minister in from England to be the church's pastor and rector. Because the church sponsored the pastor's travel to America to take a job, it violated an immigration law passed by Congress after the Civil War, which was designed to keep companies from bringing in cheap foreign labor so as to not depress the wage market for American citizens.

Holy Trinity Church was fined for the violation and eventually found itself before the Supreme Court on its appeal. The Court concluded that the law was never intended to reach Christian pastors performing services for a church, and the Court ultimately ruled that the fine was improper. As a result, the Court vacated the judgment against the church.

In coming to its conclusion, the Court went out of its way to explain why the law *could not possibly* have applied to churches and pastors, regardless of the intent of Congress. The Court stated, "No purpose of action against religion can be imputed to any legislation, state or national." And the simple reason why "no purpose of action against religion" could be imputed to any legislation passed by Congress is because, in the words of the Supreme Court, "this is a religious people" (*Holy Trinity Church*, 465).

The Supreme Court did not rest that conclusion on a mere bald declaration to that effect. Rather, the Court supported its claim by referencing dozens of historical legal documents relative to building America. The Court began its analysis with documents from the colonial era and then moved to the emergence of the new nation, and finally it reviewed the social elements that pervaded as America grew and matured.

Starting with the commission of Christopher Columbus and continuing through the births of the colonies, through the Declaration of Independence to the Constitution of the United States, and then to the constitutions of the various states, the Supreme Court in *Holy Trinity Church* traced more than four hundred years of American history. Remarkably, in all of these historical legal documents, there are no contradictions—as the Court said, "no dissonance in these declarations." They are completely consistent with one another over a period of *more than four centuries*.

Beyond that, there is "a universal language pervading them all." That language has just "one meaning." These historical legal documents, stretching over four centuries of American history, "affirm and reaffirm" that America is a religious nation—a Christian nation.

Moreover, these are "not individual sayings" or the "declarations of private persons." They are not statements gleaned from secret diaries, private letters, or utterances made in casual conversation. Rather, they are *"organic utterances*. They speak the voice of the *entire people"* (*Holy Trinity Church*, 470, emphasis added).

In addition to the organic legal documents the Court examined, it pointed to six specific elements of American culture, customs and society to support its statement that "we find everywhere a clear recognition of the same truth," that America is a Christian nation (*Holy Trinity Church*, 471).

Let's examine the six elements discussed by the Court:

1. *The Oath of Office*: All persons assuming public office are required to take an oath to support and defend the Constitution of the United States (see Constitution, Art. VI). The oath is taken on a Christian Bible and concludes with the appeal "so help me God."

While it is true that the U.S. Constitution does not require a "religious test" to hold federal office, it is interesting to note that the 1776 Constitution of Delaware *did* require such a test. Persons assuming public office in that state had to acknowledge a "faith in God the Father, and in Jesus

Christ his only Son, and the in the Holy Ghost." He further had to specifically acknowledge that "the Holy Scriptures of the Old and New Testament were given by divine inspiration" (*Holy Trinity Church*, 469-470). In fact, all of the states had a religious test for public office until the 1900s, and the colonies all supported churches financially after the Constitution was ratified.

2. *Laws Respecting the Sabbath*: Throughout the nation, laws were in effect prohibiting the conduct of business on Sunday, including the closing of courts, legislatures and similar bodies. You might even be old enough to remember the so-called "blue laws," which began disappearing in the 1970s. We still see some evidence of them today in Minnesota in the form of laws prohibiting the sale automobiles on Sunday. A similar law prohibiting the sale of liquor on Sunday was only recently repealed. Even the Constitution of the United States respects the Sabbath. Article I, Section 7 provides that the President has "ten days (Sundays excepted)" in which to act upon a bill presented to him by Congress, before such bill automatically becomes law.

3. *Churches and Religious Organizations*: Churches and religious organizations "abound in every city, town and hamlet" (*Holy Trinity Church*, 471).

4. *Charitable Organizations*: The Supreme Court pointed out that not only did Christian churches flourish in America but also that there were "a multitude of charitable organizations existing everywhere under Christian auspices" (Ibid.).

5. *Missionary Associations*: Likewise, there were missionary associations and Bible societies that enjoyed "general support, and aiming to establish Christian missions in every quarter of the globe" (Ibid.).

Here is an interesting trivia question on this topic: What was the first Bible society in America? The answer might not only shock you, but it also lays the axe squarely to the root of the idea that the United States was founded by secular men with no Christian leaning or agenda.

In the years following the adoption of the Declaration of Independence, as the war with England raged, America experienced a shortage of Bibles. The reason was that the vast majority of Bibles in America at the time were printed in England and imported to America. A Pennsylvania publisher by the name of Robert Aitken petitioned Congress for permission to print Bibles using his equipment in America. Congress approved the request and the project began in 1781.

Even though peace with England was secured by the Treaty of Paris in 1782, Aitken continued his work. On September 12, 1782, the first Bibles printed in America were released to the public. They bore the following inscription in the front:

Whereupon, Resolved, That the United States in Congress assembled...recommend this edition of the Bible to the inhabitants of the United States. (*Journals of the Continental Congress*, Vol. XXIII, September 12, 1782, 574)

In his book on American history published in 1849, historian W. P. Strickland commented on this event, saying:

Who, in view of this fact, will call into question the assertion that this is a Bible nation. Who will charge the government with indifference to religion when the first Congress of the States assumed all the rights and performed all the duties of a Bible Society long before such an institution had an existence in the world! (W. P. Strickland, *History of the American Society from Its Organization to the Present Time* [Harper and Brothers, NY: 1849], 20-21)

That's right. The shocking answer to the question is that the Congress of the United States was the first Bible society in America.

6. *Deliberative Bodies Open in Prayer*: And finally, the Supreme Court pointed out that all deliberative bodies and conventions open their sessions in prayer. While the Court did not expound on this point, it is most instructive to examine the origins of this phenomenon, at least insofar as the United States Congress is concerned, for even today, despite prayer having been scrubbed from classrooms and every other public forum, Congress begins its sessions with prayer—and in fact, there is an operating Christian chapel deep in the recesses of the U.S. Capitol building.

It was late June 1787. In the city of Philadelphia, the Constitutional Convention was in full swing, and the delegates of the colonies were meeting in private to hammer out the details of the new government. They had been at this daunting task for five or six weeks, in continuous meetings, examining and debating the nuances of every element of the various proposals and counter-proposals. But scarce little progress was being made.

Indeed, bitter arguments raged over the scope of power that should be delegated to a national government, and how the rights of the States and the people would be preserved and protected. By June 28, 1787, the convention was hopelessly deadlocked over the important question of how the states and the people were to be represented in Congress. Each state delegation was committed to its own proposal.

Not only was the work of the convention stalled, but also the New York delegation actually walked out in protest. Other state delegations were threatening to follow. The dedicated commitment to unity that was forged during the war was dissolving. The stated goal of strengthening the union—the reason for convening in the first place—might be the very thing that destroyed it.

In the midst of this crisis, Benjamin Franklin, a delegate from Pennsylvania and at age 81 by far the oldest statesman of the convention, rose to speak to the assembly. Franklin was the most prominent physicist of his age. He was a philosopher and inventor. He was one of the few founders who signed both the Declaration of Independence and the Constitution. Today, he is held out to Americans as an atheist.

Franklin's remarks were offered in the teeth of the deadlocked convention. His impromptu comments began by recognizing that the convention was struggling to find answers, no doubt due to "our own want of political wisdom." He pointed out that their lack of progress was "melancholy proof of the imperfection of the Human Understanding." From there, he put forth the following appeal, which made an everlasting imprint on Congress, even to this very day:

> In this situation of this Assembly, groping as it were in the dark to find political truth, and scarce able to distinguish it when presented to us, how has it happened, Sir, that we have not hitherto once thought of humbly applying to the Father of lights, to illuminate our understandings? In the beginning of the contest with Great Britain, when we were sensible of danger, we had daily prayer in this room for the divine protection. Our prayers, sir, were heard, and they were graciously answered. All of us who were engaged in the struggle must have observed frequent instances of a superintending Providence in our favor. To that kind Providence we owe this happy opportunity of consulting in peace on the means of establishing our future national felicity. And have we now forgotten that powerful friend? Or do we imagine that we no longer need his assistance? I have lived, Sir, a long time, and the longer I live, the more convincing proofs I see of this truth—*that God governs in the affairs of men.* And if a sparrow cannot fall to the ground without his notice, is it probable that an empire can rise without his aid? We have been assured, Sir, in the sacred writings, that "except the Lord build the house they labor in vain that build it." I firmly believe this; and I also believe that without his concurring aid we shall succeed in this political building no better than the

builders of Babel. We shall be divided by our little partial local interests; our projects will be confounded; and we ourselves shall become a reproach and byword down to future ages. And what is worse, mankind may hereafter from this unfortunate instance, despair of establishing governments by human wisdom, and leave it to chance, war, and conquest.

I therefore beg leave to move that henceforth prayers imploring the assistance of Heaven, and its blessings on our deliberations, be held in this Assembly every morning before we proceed to business, and that one or more of the clergy of this city be requested to officiate in that service. (James Madison, *The Debates in the Federal Convention of 1787, Which Framed the Constitution of the United States of America* [The Lawbook Exchange, Ltd, New Jersey, 1999], entry for June 28, 1787, 181, emphasis in original)

Let's consider Franklin's remarks carefully, especially since they came from one now widely reputed to have been an atheist. He acknowledged emphatically "that God governs the affairs of men" and made four specific references to Scriptures of both the Old and New Testaments to support his position, as follows:

a. "The Father of lights." This reference comes from James 1:17, where James explains that every good gift comes from God, whom James refers to as the "Father of heavenly lights."
b. "And if a sparrow cannot fall to the ground." This is a direct quote from Matthew 10:29, where Jesus instructs His disciples not to fear persecution but to rely on God.
c. "Except the Lord build the house they labor in vain that build it." This is a direct quote from Psalm 127:1, which teaches that all of life's work must have God at the foundation, lest it fail.

d. "We shall succeed in this political building no better than the builders of Babel." This is a direct reference to Genesis 11:1-9, where we find the story of the Tower of Babel, in which the builders were confused by God and thwarted in their attempts to build a temple to their own greatness.

I am quite sure you'll agree that it is hardly common practice for atheists to implore others to call on God through prayer for guidance in the most important of their affairs and, in the process, cite the Holy Scriptures as authority for the call not once, not twice, not three times, but *four* times.

Roger Sherman of Connecticut immediately seconded the motion. Thereafter, Congress opened all sessions with prayer to almighty God for direction and guidance in the deliberations. Interestingly, Roger Sherman was among the committee of five men—the others being Thomas Jefferson, Benjamin Franklin, John Adams and Robert R. Livingston—charged with drafting the Declaration of Independence in June 1776. Sherman was one of the few founders who, like Franklin, signed both the Declaration and the Constitution. And Sherman was one of just two delegates to the Convention of 1787 (Robert Morris of Pennsylvania the other) who signed both the Declaration and the nation's first governing document, the Articles of Confederation.

The "organic utterances" mentioned by the Supreme Court establish an unbroken chain of historical events, facts, and legal precedent that reveal the true nature of America's founding beliefs and culture. From this irrefutable history we can reach just one inescapable conclusion: *Christianity is in our DNA.*

America was in fact founded as a Christian nation by Christian people, and the universal practice of Christianity as a way of life, and as the means of informing her political, social and legal identity, is what made America great.

Generations of Americans have no idea about any of these historical facts. Christians need to know these truths to deflect the name-calling and to help build the courage they need to witness for Christ unashamedly to the people closest to them.

CHAPTER 4

America Is Losing the Culture War

We all know that Christianity is under attack at just about every turn. In political clashes throughout America, the cultural debate rages whether Christian or secular policies should dictate the answer to vexing social questions. At least partly because of our unwillingness to witness to those closest to us, America is losing the culture war. In the process, Christian principles are being driven from society.

It started as a very slow movement, but now Christianity has been scrubbed from our schools, our public councils and agencies, and from government in general. Organizations like the Freedom From Religion Foundation and the ACLU regularly bring lawsuits against local government agencies and school boards seeking to wash all vestiges of Christianity from public view.

We see this most recently and notably in the debate over whether homosexual marriage should be permitted as a matter of law or whether we should cling to the historical Judeo-Christian view of marriage as being a union between one man and one woman. As few as forty years ago, it was unimaginable to believe that the idea of a same-sex relationship would ever be sanctioned as a legal "marriage" in our society. Sure, homosexual relationships have existed since the dawn of time. During the Roman and Hellenistic periods, even up through the first century AD, such relationships were considered the norm, but so too was human slavery.

With the growth of Christianity throughout the West, homosexuality became looked upon as sin since it clearly violates God's model of marriage being between one man and one woman (see Genesis 2:19-24; Romans 1:26-27; Ephesians 5:31-33). Moreover, homosexuality, like abortion, is directly at odds with God's command that His people be fruitful and multiply. Such a thing is impossible in a same-sex relationship. Even Caesar Augustus recognized that such practices threatened the traditional culture of Rome. His series of so-called family laws were passed at his instigation over a period of about twenty years, starting roughly in 17 BC. These laws limited divorces, punished adultery (though he himself was no stranger to it), and encouraged Roman citizens to have larger families by punishing childlessness.

He most certainly didn't do so because of Christian principals. Most of these laws were passed well before Jesus lived. He did so because the libertine sexual and marital practices of the Romans were contributing to the decline of Roman culture. He saw the culture of Rome dying largely because Roman citizens were not procreating. They had no one to pass their culture to. To curb the death spiral, he passed the family laws to bring back "the practices of our ancestors that were passing in our age." Augustus intuitively recognized that a culture cannot be sustained if it is killing itself (see *De Imperatoribus Romanus*, An Encyclopedia of Roman Rulers: Augustus [Penn State University]).

In the State of Minnesota, a society steeped in Catholicism and Lutheranism for well over one hundred years, not that long ago it was impossible to imagine that same-sex relationships would ever be sanctioned by law. In fact, the legal history of the issue goes back further in Minnesota than anywhere else. The first case in the United States in which a homosexual couple sued for the right to marry occurred in Minnesota.

The case is *Baker v. Nelson*, 291 Minn. 310, 191 N.W.2d 185 (1971). That case reached the Minnesota Supreme Court in 1971. The Court ruled then that a state law limiting marriage to persons of the opposite sex did not violate the Constitution. Baker appealed, and on October 10, 1972, the Supreme Court of the United States dismissed the appeal, leaving the Minnesota Supreme Court's opinion to stand as precedent. It is fascinating to note that the Minnesota Supreme Court's reasoning, while it patterned the thinking of Augustus, was grounded in the Christian Bible. The Court stated:

> The institution of marriage as a union of man and woman, uniquely involving the procreation and rearing of children within a family, is as old as the book of Genesis. Skinner v. Oklahoma, ex rel. Williamson, [citation omitted], which invalidated Oklahoma's Habitual Criminal Sterilization Act on equal protection grounds, stated in part: "Marriage and procreation are fundamental to the very existence and survival of the race." This historic institution manifestly is more deeply founded than the asserted contemporary concept of marriage and societal interests for which petitioners contend. The due process clause of the Fourteenth Amendment is not a charter for restructuring it by judicial legislation.

At that point, the political fight was on. Responding to the state court's ruling, in June 1972, at the Minnesota Democratic–Farmer–Labor Party (DFL) State Convention, a plank was added to the party's platform supporting the idea of same-sex marriage. I believe this is the first claim of support by a major U.S. political party for same-sex marriage. But even at that, many DFL lawmakers distanced themselves from the plank because the radical stance was so far removed from the mainstream of Minnesota's (and the U.S.'s) Christian culture. That same year, Minnesota saw its first Gay Pride Festival.

Over the next forty-plus years, proponents of the cultural attack never gave up. As the Left pushed for changes to Minnesota law, amendments to the state Constitution were proposed to permanently define marriage as between one man and one woman. On May 11, 2011, the Minnesota Senate passed a bill to place a proposed amendment on the ballot. The amendment would ban same-sex marriage but allow so-called "civil unions." What happened next could never have happened in this state even just ten years before that election. The amendment was defeated, making Minnesota the first state to reject a constitutional ban on same-sex marriage.

Public opinion on the matter went from about 25 percent in support of same-sex marriage in 2000 to about 63 percent as of 2013. In 2011, when the Minnesota amendment was on the ballot, 52.6 percent of voters rejected the ban on same-sex marriage. That year also saw the *Advocate* magazine, a source for homosexual news and information, name Minneapolis the "Gayest U.S. City" (see http://www.startribune.com/gayest-city-magazine-says-it-s-minneapolis/113618049/).

In just the few short years following the 2011 vote, we've reached the point where we cannot have separate bathrooms for men and women; rather, men who "identify" as women can use a women's bathroom in a public place. And this is not just for adults. Under former President Obama, a regulation was issued under which schools were required to allow transgender students to use the bathroom that corresponds with their "gender identity." If one happened to "transition" from male to female, he was able to use the women's restroom. Those who transitioned from female to male were able to use the men's.

While President Trump withdrew those regulations, New York City schools are following Obama's lead. In May 2017, the New York City Department of Education announced that beginning in January 2018, every public school in the city must have at least one single-stall (labeled "gender-inclusive") bathroom. The decision was made specifically to countermand Trump's decision to lift Obama's regulations.

To take it even further, it seems we can't refer to boys as boys or girls as girls. In September 2017, we were treated to the story of the fifth-grade teacher in Tallahassee, Florida, who decided that she would scrub all gender-specific pronouns from both her vocabulary and that of her students. The students were no longer allowed to use terms like his, hers, he or she. Rather, they all had to use gender-neutral pronouns such as they, them, and their. She even referred to herself using a gender-neutral prefix to her name. She was not Mrs., Miss, or even Ms. She was to be referred to as "Mx"—pronounced "Mix." This couldn't be more bizarre if you made it up. (See the *USA Today* story here: https://www.usatoday.com/story/news/nation-now/2017/09/20/teacher-requests-students-use-gender-neutral-pronouns/687647001/).

As secularists wage their war on Christian heritage and culture, the courts at all levels are only too happy to oblige them, claiming that the "separation of church and state" requires that all Christian ideas, beliefs and practices be expunged from the public square. Statutes and plaques depicting the Ten Commandments are removed from public parks and courthouses. Prayer is forbidden in the classrooms of public schools and on playgrounds. Nativity scenes are evicted from public grounds. And now we can't refer to Christmas as "Christmas" but must call it the "winter holiday."

We see this in the 2014 actions of the Montgomery County Maryland public schools. On November 11, 2014, the school board voted 7-1 to remove all religious references to the district's vacation periods. Of course, the only religious references were to Christian holidays, most notably, Christmas and Easter. Thus, the Christmas holiday would no longer be shown on the school's calendar as such. Rather, it would henceforth be known as the winter holiday. Likewise, the word "Easter" would be expunged in favor of the spring holiday.

Can you imagine any of this happening twenty-five years ago?

It's happening because a growing segment of our population is unchurched. For most of our history, as I document in chapter 3, America was an overtly Christian nation made up of people who practiced their faith outwardly. Christianity was deeply entrenched in American culture. Through the first half of the twentieth century, upwards of 90 percent of Americans identified themselves as Christian (whether or not they regularly attended worship services). Consistently throughout that period, nearly 65 percent of all Americans regularly attended a weekly Christian church service of some kind.

Studies conducted in 2004 and 2005 show that those numbers are now much lower. The latter study, published in *The Journal for the Scientific Study of Religion* by sociologists C. Kirk Hadaway and Penny Long Marler, reveals that the number of people worshiping each week is fewer than 20 percent. While the actual figure may be a revelation, the fact that church attendance has been dropping steadily is not. Over the past thirty to forty years, all mainstream Christian denominations have reported net losses in church attendance.

And if church attendance is dropping, it should come as no surprise that the number of Americans identifying themselves as Christians is also dropping. A 2015 Gallup poll showed that the number of those calling themselves Christians (whether or not they attended church regularly) was just 75.2 percent. That number itself was down from 80.1 percent in 2008. At the same time, the number of people claiming to have no ties to religion went up by 5 percent, to nearly 20 percent of our population. Moreover, as of 2015, 5 percent of our population claims to be associated with non-Christian religions.

A key reason for that is the growth of Islam in the U.S. The Pew Research Center tells us that the number of Muslim immigrants, as well as natural-born U.S. citizens claiming to be Muslim, is growing steadily. As of 2015, 1 percent of the U.S. population (currently about 322 million people) associated themselves with Islam. Pew expects that number to double by 2020. Pew further projects that before 2040, Muslims will become the second largest religious group in the U.S., behind Christians. Pew claims that Islam is the fastest growing religion in the world, including in America. Pew's analysis says that between 2020 and 2046, Islam will grow twice as fast as the world's population growth and, by the second half of this century, will replace Christianity as the world's largest religion (see http://www.pewresearch.org/fact-tank/2017/04/06/why-muslims-are-the-worlds-fastest-growing-religious-group/).

We already see this kind of growth in the Twin Cities. According to church demographer Dr. John A. Mayer, the first Muslim immigrants settled in the area in 1946. By 1999, Islam became the second most common religion in the Twin Cities, behind only Christianity, and surpassing Judaism (see Mayer, *Cityview Report, Strategic Data for Effective Ministry*, 16th edition, 2015). The growth of Islam is attributed mostly to the large influx of Somali refugees that started in 1993. Today, the Twin Cities has the largest Somali population in America. In 2006, Minneapolis elected the first Muslim to Congress in the person of Keith Ellison. He took his oath of office on a Quran.

The decline of Christianity started in the late 1960s and has continued to this day, though the rate of decline has picked up speed during this century. I don't think it's any accident that this started at exactly the time that both prayer and Bible reading were removed from public schools by order of the Supreme Court. In 1962, the Court declared prayer (even voluntary, non-compulsory prayer) in public schools to be a violation of the First Amendment. That case was *Engel v. Vitale*, 370 U.S. 421 (1962). Then, in 1963, in the case of *Abington School District v. Schempp*, 374 U.S. 203 (1963), the Supreme Court decided by a vote of 8–1 that school-sponsored Bible reading in public schools was unconstitutional.

In *Abington School District*, the decision of the Court turned not on legal precedent but upon the expert testimony of a historian, Dr. Solomon Grayzel. His testimony was summarized by the Court as follows:

But if portions of the New Testament were read without explanation, they could be, and, in his specific experience with children,

Dr. Grayzel observed, had been, psychologically harmful to the child, and had caused a divisive force within the social [culture] of the school. (374 U.S. at 209)

Why Dr. Grayzel's testimony about what the potential "psychological" effects of Bible reading might be on children was probative evidence is questionable since he was no psychologist or psychiatrist. He was a historian. But one has to wonder how reading both Old and New Testament scriptures can psychologically harm a child. Upon continued reading of such scriptures, a child might come away with the notions that he should:

- Respect the property of other people,
- Not engage in adultery,
- Respect the institution of marriage between one man and one woman,
- Not murder or harm another person, and
- Love his neighbor as himself.

Imagine how society might be affected if we all believed that. Indeed, one of the earlier Supreme Court precedents ignored by the Court in reaching this decision was its prior decision in the case of *Vidal v. Girard's Executors*, 43 U.S. 126 (1844). There, the eminent Justice Joseph Story delivered the opinion of the court, which directly addressed Bible reading in school. Justice Story stated:

Why may not the Bible, and especially the New Testament, without note or comment, be read and taught as a divine revelation in the college—its general precepts expounded, its evidences explained, and its glorious principles of morality inculcated? * * * Where can the purest principles of morality be learned so clearly or so perfectly as from the New Testament? Where are benevolence, the love of truth, sobriety, and industry, so powerfully and irresistibly inculcated as in the sacred volume? (43 U.S. at 200)

As to the *Engel* case, amazingly, the Court acknowledged that its decision there was not supported by a *single legal precedent*. And in fact, the Court rejected a long line of legal precedents acknowledging that local school boards, made up largely of Christian parents of the very children who attended those schools, had the authority to adopt such practices.

As a direct result of *Engel* and *Abington School District*, our young people are not being fed God's Word in the one institution in which they spend more time than any other place outside the home—their primary schools. It's not just that the Left has managed to wash Christianity out of the schools. They have introduced doctrines contrary to God's Word on an ongoing basis. Many of our young people have come to believe that Christianity is just another religion, no better or worse than any other, and certainly not deserving of any greater social respect or deference than, say, Islam or Buddhism. As such, our young people easily accept, among many other things, the idea that "diversity" and "inclusion" necessarily requires the marginalization of God's social plan, including, for example, the elimination of God's plan for marriage.

So what happens when you drive God and God's Word out of the culture? The result is that crime rages, street gangs proliferate, respect for life and property shrinks rapidly, the drug culture flourishes—bringing with it the pain of addiction and broken families. Prostitution is everywhere, and more babies are born out of wedlock now than at any other time in our history. When you take God off our streets and out of our schools, you end up with godless streets and godless schools. This is the reason that our nation's cities are burning. For example, in 1995, the once peaceful Phillips neighborhood of south Minneapolis was dubbed "Baby Beirut" because of the non-stop gunfire, street gangs, arson, drug trafficking, and prostitution. It got so bad that, in January 1997, a group of about

100 concerned citizens confronted then-Mayor Sharon Sayles Belton, demanding a house-by-house sweep to end the crime or they would ask President Clinton to declare Phillips a federal disaster area. A *Washington Post* article from January 5, 1997, describes the scope of the problems the residents of Phillips faced:

> Across the street, a steady procession of drug deals is going down on the front stoop; three or four an hour, even in the dead of winter. It's worse in the summer, when Park Avenue becomes a 24-hour bazaar of open-air prostitution, curbside drug dealing and drive-by shootings. About the only thing not visible . . . is a police officer putting a stop to any of this. (See-https://www.washingtonpost.com/archive/politics/1997/01/05/steady-reign-of-crime-has-neighborhood-hoping-for-disaster-relief/7b51fc67-c5d8-4d16-8296-3c39e65da5a2/?utm_term=.41fe8ac42ed6.)

The problem of godless cities was never more apparent than in the two examples of the street riots we witnessed in Ferguson, Missouri, and Baltimore, Maryland. Buildings were burned, stores were looted, cars were destroyed, and honest, innocent citizens were endangered by the lawless, violent acts of hundreds of rioters. It was a heart-breaking scene of moral and legal bankruptcy in a nation built on God's moral and legal foundation.

In a news conference after the April 2015 firestorm that gripped Baltimore, then-Baltimore Police Chief Anthony Betts responded to allegations that the police were not doing enough to quell the violence and protect innocent citizens and their property. His response was chilling. It speaks louder and more clearly than anything else possibly can about the condition of our culture as Christian principles are declared irrelevant and God is pushed further to the side every day.

Chief Betts said that the police were doing all they could under the circumstances, but given the sheer number of rioters in the streets, Betts said, "We were outnumbered and outflanked."

Think about that statement for a moment. Repeat it in your mind.

"We were outnumbered and outflanked."

When we scrub God out of our schools, and God off the streets, and God off our playgrounds—we get godless schools, godless streets, and godless playgrounds. *We get a godless society.* And when we have a godless society, we simply cannot put enough police officers on the streets to maintain order.

The great experiment in American self-government only works when people respect the law, the property, and the rights of other people. George Washington cautioned America on that very point in his farewell address to the nation on September 19, 1796, when he stated:

Of all the dispositions and habits which lead to political prosperity, religion and morality are indispensable supports. In vain would that man claim the tribute of patriotism, who should labor to subvert these great pillars of human happiness, these firmest props of the duties of men and citizens. The mere politician, equally with the pious man, ought to respect and to cherish them. A volume could not trace all their connections with private and public felicity. Let it simply be asked: Where is the security for property, for reputation, for life, if the sense of religious obligation desert the oaths which are the instruments of investigation in courts of justice? And let us with caution indulge the supposition that morality can be maintained without religion. Whatever may be conceded to the influence of refined education on minds of peculiar structure, reason and experience both forbid us to expect that national morality can prevail in exclusion of religious principle. (See Washington's address here: http://www.ushistory.org/documents/farewelladdress.htm.)

As we have scrubbed religious principal from our society, why are we surprised that our national morality has disappeared? Such morality comes only through an understanding of God, the Great Lawgiver, and the teachings of His Son, Jesus.

CHAPTER 5

The World Has Come to Us

Jesus took a broader view of Gideon's first mission. While Gideon was pushed to destroy the false idols in his own family and restore proper worship there, Jesus implored us to make disciples of all nations (see Matthew 28:19). The Hebrew word for "nations" is translated in the New Testament as "Gentiles" or "heathens." Thus, Jesus is making it clear that we are to bring the Word of God to all peoples—across the world.

As I explained in chapter 3, the Church took this command to heart in a big way by sending Christian missionaries across the globe. Virtually every part of the world has been touched by missionaries determined to make disciples, baptize them into the death and resurrection of Jesus Christ, and teach them God's Word (see Matthew 28:19-20).

This is not a top-down process. Missionaries rarely work at a national or even a regional level, speaking to thousands of people at a time. They work with small groups in villages and hamlets. By planting churches, schools and hospitals in these places, they are able to bring the Word of God to people, one family at a time. So while a missionary may be working in a remote place halfway across the world, he is nevertheless spreading the gospel, household by household. This is no different than what God commanded Gideon to do.

Most of us have never been missionaries. Most of us, including me, have never even been on a missions trip. Churches regularly sponsor such trips, of late, to places like Haiti and New Orleans, to help with disaster relief. But it's just not necessary to go across the globe, or even across the country, to make disciples of all the nations.

Throughout the nineteenth and twentieth centuries, the bulk of American immigrants came from Europe. These people were primarily Christians. While they brought with them a vast array of local customs, languages, traditions and culture, they worshiped the risen Savior, Jesus Christ. The melting pot blended this mix into a unique people with a common belief in Christianity. As I documented in chapter 3 with my discussion of the Supreme Court's decision in the case of *Holy Trinity Church v. United States*, the culture of America and its people was decidedly Christian, contrary to what the Left might have you believe today.

That pattern of immigration is no longer the case. In 2015, India and China overtook Mexico as the leading countries of origin for citizens migrating to the U.S. Behind Mexico is the Philippines. In addition to the normal flow of immigration, in the past twenty years or so, we've seen a substantial increase in the number of refugees coming to America from various war-torn parts of the world. Nearly 100,000 refugees were admitted to the U.S. in 2016 alone, 22 percent more than in 2015. The primary countries of origin for these people were the Democratic Republic of the Congo, Syria, Myanmar, Iraq, and Somalia. However, people also came in droves from Bhutan, Iran, Afghanistan, Ukraine, and Eritrea. People from these ten countries totaled 91 percent of all refugee arrivals to the U.S. in 2016 (see https://www.migrationpolicy.org/article/frequently-requested-statistics-immigrants-and-immigration-united-states).

The questions for this discussion are not whether these people should or should not be allowed to relocate to America, nor whether and to what extent U.S. immigration policy should be revised. My point is much simpler than that: no longer do Christians in America have to travel to the remotest reaches of the world to reach unchurched people. The world has come to us.

The influx of these non-Christian people groups is changing radically the demographics of our cities. Let me give you just one example: the City of Minneapolis, and in particular, the Phillips neighborhood. Beginning in the mid-nineteenth century, Phillips was home to a mix of eastern and northern European immigrants. By the 1950s, Phillips was a blue-collar, working-class neighborhood with a mix of European descendants, Native Americans, and African Americans, the latter of whom began migrating to the area from the south after the Civil War. These people worked on the railroads and in the flower mills of Minneapolis. Phillips was also home to Northwestern Hospital (now Abbott Northwestern), which opened in 1887, and Phillips was the world headquarters of Honeywell until the 1990s. Streetcars followed main routes across Lake Street and Franklin Avenues, the main east-west arteries through the heart of the neighborhood, just south of downtown Minneapolis. Industrial and commercial activity thrived for the shops, restaurants and businesses lining Lake Street.

That was then. This is now.

The groundbreaking work of Dr. John Mayer shows a completely different picture for Phillips today. Besides the crime issues I addressed in chapter 4, in 1996, Phillips was dubbed the Ellis Island of Minnesota because of the high number of immigrants and refugees settling there. In 2003, Phillips became the single most diverse neighborhood in America, with more than one hundred languages spoken there. Today, Minneapolis's light rail system sells tickets in four languages on the routes that pass through Phillips. A short distance from Phillips we find a major north-south thoroughfare called Nicolette Avenue. There are seventy-five ethnic restaurants within a six-block stretch on Nicolette, which is known as "Eat Street."

In his article "The Great Commission in Reverse," Dr. Mayer explains the scope of change brought about by the influx of non-Christian immigrants. He says:

> Eleven church buildings in the Twin Cities have now become mosques. There are plans to build the largest mosque in America in Minneapolis and it will cost $48 million. This new "megamosque" in Minneapolis will be right near an apartment complex nicknamed "Vertical Africa" where currently 5,000 Muslims live. The Twin Cities is also home to the largest Cambodian Buddhist temple in America as well as the largest Hindu temple in North America. (John Mayer, "The Great Commission in Reverse," *Global Missiology Journal*, January 2015, p. 9)

According to Dr. Mayer's research, 337,000 people were involved in world religious worship in 315 mosques, temples or home settings in the Twin Cities. This includes:

- 161,000 Muslims meeting in 132 mosques or other settings,
- 72,500 Buddhists meeting in 84 temples or home settings,
- 42,500 Hindus meeting in 37 different temples or other settings, and
- Thousands of other miscellaneous religious groups, such as Confucianists, Sikhs and Jains, to name a few.

Add to that, there are 20,000 witches who meet in 303 groups throughout the area, one of the highest concentrations in the U.S. We also have eight homosexual churches in the Twin Cities. The Twin Cities also has the nation's highest concentration of Hmongs (90,000), Somalis (77,000), and Liberians (37,500). We also host 32,000 Chinese and 26,000 Vietnamese immigrants.

This phenomenon is by no means peculiar to the Twin Cities. Major cities throughout the nation are experiencing the same thing. Consider the following:

- Chicago has the second largest Serbian population of any city in the world, with over 500,000 living there.
- Detroit is the largest Muslim city in America, with an Arab population of 405,000, an Iraqi population of 100,000, and 22,000 Yeminis.
- New York City is known as Little Pakistan with 120,000 Pakistanis residents.
- The San Francisco Bay Area hosts 65,000 Afghans along with 300,000 Chinese.
- St. Louis has the largest population of Bosnians in America at 75,000.
- Nashville has the most Kurds of any city in America with 11,000 residents.
- Miami is the second largest Haitian city in the world. (Mayer, "The Great Commission in Reverse," p. 5)

This list could go on and on, but one thing is crystal clear: The world has come to us as never before.

Since "The Great Commission in Reverse" was published in 2015, the number of former church buildings that have been converted to mosques has reached sixteen. In addition, nine former churches have become Buddhist temples, four were sold to become Hindu temples, and one former church is now a Sikh temple. Now, you might ask how it is that thirty church buildings in Minneapolis became mosques or temples. The answer is that since 1970, seventy-eight churches moved out of the city and relocated to the suburbs. They sold off their buildings to the highest bidders.

This makes me wonder: Is the church on the move? Or is the church on the *run*?

These facts contribute greatly to the problem I discuss in chapter 4, that Christianity is losing the culture war in America. But with every problem comes a great opportunity. In fact, great accomplishments are always the birth child of great opportunities. In this case, the opportunity is that the harvest field is vast and ripe. It is right before our eyes, and in many cases all we have to do is walk out the front door.

Some may recoil at the numbers I cite here and react in fear. They may cry loudly (or in some cases, louder) for immigration reform to stop the flow. I don't write this to make any kind of case for immigration reform at any level. The fact is, that ship has sailed. The people of the world are already here—and they brought their world religions with them. The question for Christians is whether we are going to run from it or deal with it as Christ would have us do. To this point in time, we've been running from it, as is indicated by the flight of churches from the city.

But if we take Jesus' command to go out into the world to preach the gospel, and the Church did just that for centuries, why would we shrink from that duty now, when the world has come to us? In fact, in the case of many of the people groups that are now living among us, it would have been impossible for Christian missionaries to go to them. Dr. Mayer makes a very sobering observation regarding this fact, pointing to two people groups prevalent in the Phillips neighborhood: Somalis and Tibetans. He notes:

> Even if you are called to reach Somalis in Somalia you can't. You can't get a visa to travel and even if you sneak across the border illegally into Somalia, you can't eat camel burgers with them, play soccer with them, and share the gospel. No, instead you will most likely by killed or kidnapped. Tibet is a similar story, where the Dalai Lama himself cannot return to Tibet. (Mayer, "The Great Commission in Reverse," p. 11)

The conclusion drawn by Dr. Mayer seems inescapable. Since Christians cannot go to so many of the places in the world that are oppressed by ungodly governments and false religions, God in His wisdom and mercy *brought them here*. This mass of lost people is at our doorsteps. They live in our neighborhoods. They go to our schools. They work where we work. They have become our neighbors. We have a duty to love our neighbors and to be salt and light to them. And you don't have to travel across the globe to do it.

CHAPTER 6

It's Time to Show Up for Work

Have you ever applied for a job? Imagine with me that you're in the process of submitting an application for your dream job. You craft your résumé very carefully, taking pains to list your background, skills, training education and experience. You pour over every word diligently, being sure there are no typos or silly grammatical errors. You send off the résumé with a prayer that it will find its way to a person with an open mind.

After a time, you get word that you've been selected for an interview. The excitement and anticipation grow as you prepare for your first face-to-face meeting. You review your résumé again and probably even rehearse answers to a few anticipated questions. Finally, you put together a list of your best references in the hope that the interview goes to the next step.

Now comes the day of your meeting. In the morning, you shine yourself up and put on your best suit or dress. You make doublesure you leave the house in plenty of time to get to the meeting with a few minutes to spare. There could be no worse message to send a prospective new employer than to be late for your first job interview.

At the meeting you conduct yourself as the consummate professional. You are polite, respectful, and you use your best communication skills. You make sure you don't use any vulgar language or social media lingo in your discussions. You make every effort to put your best foot forward in every way. You even turn off your cell phone! You try to communicate clearly who you are, your level of skill and experience, and that you are the best person for the job.

You leave the interview feeling confident.

Then before long, you get a phone call—with the good news. You've been hired for the job. You are to start next Monday. You are elated. All the time and effort in crafting your résumé and rehearsing for the interview paid off. You feel a great sense of joy and relief. You're getting your dream job after all. You go to bed Sunday night with great anticipation.

But Monday morning comes and, to your shock, it turns out your alarm didn't go off. You overslept! You're two hours late and it's the first day. Rather than get to work with half the day already gone, you decide to call your boss and explain. "Sorry, boss," you say with great contrition. "The alarm didn't go off. I'll be in early tomorrow."

You roll out of bed Tuesday morning with the greatest upset stomach ever. "It must be the stress," you say to yourself. "Or it could be the flu bug." You remember your neighbor complaining about it just last week. You reason that you can't take the chance of getting all your new colleagues sick on your first day, so you call the boss again. "Sorry, boss. I'm sick. I can't make it in. But don't worry. I'll be there tomorrow, for sure."

Wednesday morning comes. You feel great and leap out of bed with staunch determination. You didn't even need the alarm clock. You take a quick shower, gobble some breakfast and head to the car with a spring in your step. You jump in the car and turn the key. Click—nothing. The battery is dead. The car won't start. And now for the third day in a row, you have to call your boss, explain the situation and promise that you'll be there tomorrow, even if the stars fall from the sky.

How many days do you think this could continue before you don't have a job? I have to believe that after just the first time the boss would have kindly told you to forget it, that he will move in another direction.

I want you to think about this in the context of your faith. Becoming a Christian is much like being hired by God. Your salvation makes you a part of the team. Then there's the next step.

In Matthew chapters 5–7, Jesus presents the Sermon on the Mount. He starts His teaching with the Beatitudes. He tells us that the blessed among us are:

- The poor in spirit for theirs is the kingdom of heaven,
- They who mourn as they will be comforted,
- The meek since they will inherit the earth,
- Those who hunger and thirst for righteousness for they will be filled,
- The merciful as they will be shown mercy,
- The pure in heart as they will see God,
- The peacemakers as they will be called the children of God, and
- They who are persecuted, insulted, and spoken of falsely by others because of righteousness and for following Jesus, because to them belongs the kingdom of heaven (see Matthew 5:3-11).

I'm sure you noticed that each of these is a specific characteristic of a person's heart. They are personality traits. They speak directly to how a person is expected to act toward his fellow man. You might say that Jesus is describing here the ideal attributes of a Christian and a Christian's heart. You might go so far as to say that these are the job requirements God is looking for on the résumé.

Lucky for us, God does not hire off the résumé. If He did, none of us would get the job. We are all imperfect. At one level or another, to a greater or lesser extent, we have all sinned (see Romans 3:23). That sin separates us from God. And without atonement for sin, mankind remains separated from God. We are, so to speak, off the team.

But regardless of your weaknesses, your failures, your personal deficiencies, you can enjoy fellowship and communion with God. The shed blood of Christ atoned for all sin, and the blessing of atonement is that you are able to have communion with God. It is offered as a free gift. In Romans 3:24, Paul makes it clear that salvation is offered by God freely, through His grace and mercy. It is received by us through faith in Jesus. Thus, it is the shed blood of Christ alone that atones for our sin and allows for our redemption. Without that, none of us would ever get hired.

When you make your confession of faith in Christ, your sin is forgiven. You are redeemed. It's like getting hired for a new job, and this time God is your boss. Now, what's next? It seems to me, you have to show up for work. And with the world at our doorstep, there's never been a better time to do it.

Jesus makes this very point in Matthew chapter 5, verses 13-16. Now that you've been saved—that is, you've been hired for the job and you're on the team—this is the next step. God expects you to show up for work and produce for His glory. Jesus says:

> You are the salt of the earth. But if the salt loses its saltiness, how can it be made salty again? It is no longer good for anything, except to be thrown out and trampled underfoot. You are the light of the world. A town built on a hill cannot be hidden. Neither do people light a lamp and put it under a bowl. Instead they put it on its stand, and it gives light to everyone in the house. In the same way, let your light shine before others, that they may see your good deeds and glorify your Father in heaven. (Matthew 5:13-16, NIV)

There is no question in my mind but that this is the *practical application* of the beatitudes. The beatitudes speak to the inward condition of one's heart. As I said, they are personality traits, if you will. The act of being salt and light to the world around us is the outward manifestation of those inward personality traits. In other words, being salt and light is the process of putting your faith into action, a key element of the Christian walk.

James, the brother of Jesus, makes this point clearly in his letter to the church. He states, in chapter 2, verse 17, that faith without works is dead. "What good is it?" he asks very poignantly, if a brother comes to you in need of food or clothing, and your response to him is simply, "Go in peace; be warm and well fed." Does that solve the brother's problems of being hungry or naked? Of course not.

James rightly declares that we show our faith through our actions. Note that we are not *saved* by our actions. Christ alone saves us. He alone makes us righteous (see Romans 3:22). But once we receive that gift of salvation—once we're hired for the job of God's emissary on Earth—we are expected to show up for work. As James points out, our faith and actions must work together (see James 2:22).

Peter also makes it clear that our faith cannot stand alone. God expects personal growth and action. In 2 Peter 1:5-7, he explains that we must add to our faith. To faith we must add goodness, and to goodness, we add knowledge. And from there we are to add self-control, perseverance, godliness, mutual affection, and love. This is a tall order, to be sure. It is undertaken, as Peter says, to keep "from being ineffective and unproductive in your knowledge of our Lord Jesus Christ" (2 Peter 1:8, NIV).

This is the essential teaching of Jesus himself, as set forth in Matthew 25:34-40. As we do for the least of those around us—the poor, the naked, the wretched—we do for Christ himself.

It is clear to me, therefore, that the call to be salt and light is, in fact, a call to action. That is, the terms are used as verbs, not nouns. Stated more simply, to carry out this command we need to get off the couch.

CHAPTER 7

What Is Salt?

In Matthew 5:13, Jesus says, "You are the salt of the earth."

Salt had great value in the ancient world. Indeed, salt was the single most precious spice of that time, and one of the most valuable of all commodities. So valuable was it that it was used as currency in many ways, much like gold and silver. For example, in the very early years of the Roman Republic (pre-Empire), Roman soldiers were paid, at least partially, in salt. The Latin word for "salt," *salaria*, is where we get our word "salary," which, of course, is compensation for services rendered. It is said that we get the word "soldier" from *sal dare*, meaning "to give salt."

Due to the high value of salt, an ancient Roman proverb said that people who did their job well were "worth their salt." On the other hand, a slave of little value was not worth his salt. In ancient Rome, people along the seashore created ponds to allow salt water to warm under the Mediterranean sun. The sun evaporated the water, allowing the pure sea salt to be gathered and sold. Any person who had such a pond of his own was often among the wealthiest in the area. Venice rose to great economic power because of its capacity to harvest and transport salt throughout the Mediterranean region.

In its 1982 article "A Brief History of Salt," *Time* magazine editors provided the following insight:

Salt routes crisscrossed the globe. One of the most traveled led from Morocco south across the Sahara to Timbuktu. Ships bearing salt from Egypt to Greece traversed the Mediterranean and the Aegean. Herodotus describes a caravan route that united the salt oases of the Libyan Desert. Venice's glittering wealth was attributable not so much to exotic spices as to commonplace salt, which Venetians exchanged in Constantinople for the spices of Asia. In 1295, when he first returned from Cathay, Marco Polo delighted the Doge with tales of the prodigious value of salt coins bearing the seal of the great Khan. (http://content.time.com/time/magazine/article/0,9171,925341,00.html)

Of all the roads that spoked out of the city of Rome to the far reaches of the empire, the Via Salaria—the salt road—was among the busiest and most important. It started at the mouth of the Tiber river west of Rome. It was from there that much of the salt used in the city was harvested. The road stretched just about due east to Castrum Truentinum (currently called Porto d'Ascoli) on the coast of the Adriatic. Roman soldiers used the road along with merchants who brought the precious spice to the city from both the east and the west.

Salt was extremely valuable for at least three reasons:

First, it was a preservative. Of course there was no refrigeration in the first century, making long-term food preservation tenuous at best. Salt was used to preserve meat and fish, preventing rot and decay. This was the case with salt right through the mid-nineteenth century, when electricity and refrigeration become prevalent. Salt was one of the most effective means of preserving food, making the crystals highly coveted for that reason alone.

While salt is certainly not as valuable today, it still functions as an important preservative. Just read the label on any processed food package. Salt is the primary ingredient, used expressly for the purpose of retarding decay. The sodium draws water out of the food to reduce potential bacterial activity, thus increasing the viability of the product for long periods of time.

The second reason salt was so valuable is because it is a disinfectant. It was used for medicinal purposes. Roman soldiers applied salt to open wounds to disinfect them and speed the healing process. Anyone who's ever gone swimming in the ocean with a cut knows how quickly a cut heals after being exposed to sea salt. Israelite midwives always bathed newborn babies in salt as part of the cleaning process (see Ezekiel 16:4). The Romans, steeped in paganism, had a god or goddess for everything. The goddess of health or well-being was Salus. The root of the name, *sal*, derives from the Latin word for salt.

Today we know that sea salt has profound health benefits. There are dozens of nutrients available from the minerals in seawater. These minerals are essential for the healthy function of the body. The minerals in sea salt include sodium, potassium, fluoride, calcium, magnesium, bromide, chloride, iron, copper, and zinc, just to name a few. Sea salt is added to hundreds of various health and beauty products because of its vast array of beneficial properties.

Finally, salt was a spice. It was used to season food, to make it more palatable. We do the same today. No cook "worth his salt" would operate a kitchen without plenty of sea salt on hand at all times. It's perhaps the one spice that is simply indispensable in the preparation of any type of cuisine. In fact, of all the various spices, salt is probably the one ingredient singularly responsible for giving our food its desirable taste. And at that, it generally takes but a pinch or two to achieve the desired result.

When Jesus commanded us to be the salt of the earth, I'm sure He had all three of these attributes in mind. If you are going to be the salt of the earth, you have to be a preservative, a disinfectant, and a spice. Let's explore just how we might apply all three of these attributes to daily life.

CHAPTER 8

Christians as a Preservative

In 1790, Benjamin Franklin wrote a stern letter to an individual who sought the wise man's opinion on a treatise he wrote. The treatise harshly criticized and showed open hostility toward Christianity. Some believe the letter was written to Thomas Paine, whose book *The Age of Reason*, did exactly that. While we are not certain of the recipient, Franklin's message to the would-be author about attacking Christianity in America is certain. Franklin encouraged the man in the strongest terms to use his talents to tackle some other subject. Franklin's letter reads in part:

> You might easily display your excellent talents of reasoning on a less hazardous subject, and thereby obtain rank with our most distinguished authors. For among us, it is not necessary, as among the Hottentots that a youth to be received into the Company of Men, should prove his manhood by beating his mother. *I would advise you therefore not to attempt unchaining the Tiger, but to burn this piece before it is seen by any other person*, whereby you will save yourself a great deal of mortification from the enemies it may raise against you, and perhaps a good deal of regret and repentance. *If men are so wicked as we now see them with religion what would they be if without it?* (William Temple Franklin, *The Works of Benjamin Franklin*, 1817, vol. VI, pp. 243-244, emphasis added)

From my discussion in chapter 4 about the condition of the Phillips neighborhood, it's pretty easy to see what men become when we scrub God and His Word from our culture. When that happens, the culture regresses to a time when there was no restraint over personal vices and precious little respect for life and property. Ever since the Christian worldview took hold in the first century, a new level of respect for life and property was born and matured. We must work to *preserve* the Christian worldview if there's ever to be stability and security in our society.

The Romans had little regard for life. In fact, throughout the world at that time, there was little regard for life. For example, Roman fathers were the ultimate arbiter over whether a newborn child lived or died. When a child was born, the midwife laid it at the father's feet. If he picked it up, the child lived. If he did not, it was often just left to die or otherwise was sold as property. Females were held in particularly low regard as women were considered mere property to begin with.

Slavery was a common practice everywhere in the world. The Romans elevated slavery to an art form. And Roman slavery had nothing whatsoever to do with race. Romans held slaves from every corner of the world that they dominated. That included North Africa from the far west coast all the way to Egypt. It included the entirety of Europe north to the British Isles. The Roman Empire stretched east to encompass all of Greece, Turkey and Palestine, as well as north through the Balkans. Many of the conquered people were brought back to Rome as slaves. By the time of Christ's birth, the city of Rome had a population of about one million people, and about 25 percent were slaves.

It was the Christian influence on the people of the west that introduced, for the first time anywhere, any level of respect for life and property. This was done by spreading the Word of God throughout the countryside. The Word has the effect of stopping rot, decay and corruption. The Word acts as a preservative to ensure life and peace, which in turn brings prosperity.

Nowhere in the world did God's Word take deeper root, and produce greater fruit, than in America, as discussed in chapter 3. This fact was documented through the work of Alexis de Tocqueville of France. De Tocqueville was a French jurist, political philosopher, and sociologist. Beginning in April 1831, he spent ten months traveling throughout America. His purpose was to study our nation's legal and penal system with an eye toward understanding how it was that America so quickly became such a great nation in just the few short decades since the adoption of its Constitution in 1789.

De Tocqueville's findings were published in 1840 in a book entitled *Democracy in America*. For decades, *Democracy in America* was high on the list of required reading in American colleges and universities in subjects including political science, history, sociology, and even literature. The reasons include the remarkable thoroughness of de Tocqueville's analysis of the American legal system and his independent analysis of American culture.

His conclusions are grounded exclusively on his vast personal experiences and firsthand observations. Thus, *Democracy in America* is not so much a history book of America as it is "an eloquent essay in timely reality stopped at a point in time" ("Notes from the Editors," *Democracy in America*, The Legal Classics Library [Birmingham, AL:Gryphon Editions, Inc., 1988], p. 14).

In his book, De Tocqueville discussed America's Christian culture at length. He noted that Christianity, more than any other factor, shaped the political views of Americans. It defined their views on liberty, government, and the power of law. It formed the foundations of their personal lives, their marriages, and their families. It dictated their public manners and moral code. He even referred to Christianity as the "foremost of the political institutions" in America because "it facilitates the free use of institutions" (*Democracy in America*, p. 286).

De Tocqueville observed that the first thing that impressed him upon his arrival in America was the country's strong, overarching Christian culture. He noted that "Christianity reigns without any obstacle, *by universal consent*" (*Democracy in American*, p. 286, emphasis added).

He observed:

> The Americans combine the notions of Christianity and of liberty so intimately in their minds, that it is impossible to make them conceive the one without the other (*Democracy in America*, p. 287).

By the end of the nineteenth century, America was a leading industrial and manufacturing power in the world. She developed and invented at a remarkable pace. With just 5 percent of the world's land mass and about 6 percent of the world's population, America produced half of just about everything produced in the world: food, textiles, housing, mining, communication, transportation, electricity, commodities, luxury goods—*everything*. She exported her bounty across the globe and, as such, was a creditor nation.

More important, her economic model and political freedom were responsible for lifting more people out of poverty further and faster than any other nation in the history of the world. In fact, no other nation on Earth enjoyed the level of liberty that Americans did. Because of that, standards of living were raised for everybody, and national wealth increased as never before—*anywhere* in the world (see Morison, Commager, Leuchtenburg, *The Growth of the American Republic*, 7th Edition, Vol. II [NY: Oxford University Press, 1980], pp. 50-52).

How did we get so great so fast? De Tocqueville observed that the people of America shared a conviction that "their country is unlike any other, and that its situation is without precedent in the world." He referred to America as a "land of wonders" in which anything was possible, and that if something was not yet done, it is only because "it was not yet attempted" (*Democracy in America*, p. 405).

At the core of it all was America's *universal* Christian faith that preserved life and liberty and led to prosperity. Consider this remarkable observation by de Tocqueville about the level of influence Christianity had on American culture:

> [T]here is no country in the whole world, in which the Christian religion retains a greater influence over the souls of men than in America; and there can be no greater proof of its utility, and of its conformity to human nature, than that its influence is most powerfully felt over the most enlightened and free nation of the earth. (*Democracy in America*, pp. 284-285)

As to the true source of America's greatness, de Tocqueville is credited with this poignant and poetic observation:

> I sought for the greatness and genius of America in her commodious harbors and her ample rivers, and it was not there; in her fertile fields and boundless prairies, and it was not there; in her rich mines and her vast world commerce, and it was not there. Not until I went into the churches of America and heard her pulpits aflame with righteousness did I understand the secret of her genius and power. America is great because America is good, and if America ever ceases to be good, America will cease to be great. (Ezra Taft Benson, *God, Family, Country: Our Three Great Loyalties* [Salt Lake City, UT: Desert Book Co., 1975], p. 360; Robert Flood, *The Rebirth of America* [The Arthur S. DeMoss Foundation, 1986], p. 32)

If we are to *preserve* this greatness in our nation and pass it on to our children, then we have a responsibility to talk to those around us about Jesus. We have to introduce people to His saving grace, which is the only true preservative for life. As Jesus said to the Samaritan woman at the well, "whoever drinks the water I give them will never thirst" (John 4:14) What a preservative that is!

Moreover, you have no idea what impact your testimony might have on another person's life. You don't know who's listening to you or how a given person will run with God's Word. Let me illustrate.

Without question, one of the greatest evangelists in the history of the world was Peter. Peter was handpicked by Jesus to lead the early church. And after Peter's failures made him stronger, his evangelism through the Holy Spirit was responsible for lighting the fire that spread Christianity to the world. So let's ask the question: how did Peter learn about Jesus in the first place? The story is rarely discussed but is profoundly important.

The story is told in John 1:35-40. Peter's brother, Andrew, was a disciple of John the Baptist. As John the Baptist was walking with Andrew and another of John's disciples, John saw Jesus passing by. John said to the two men with him, "Look, the Lamb of God" (John 1:36). The two then followed Jesus and spent the day with Him.

The next thing Andrew did was to find his brother. Andrew told Peter, "We have found the Messiah" (John 1:41). That is, *Andrew* told Peter about Jesus. He then brought Peter to Jesus to meet Him personally (see John 1:42). At that meeting Jesus anointed Peter as His disciple. Peter went on to become one of the world's greatest evangelists. Interestingly, we hear nothing further about Andrew, but what remarkable fruit Andrew produced by telling *one person* about Christ.

The lesson bears repeating: as you talk about Christ, you don't know who's listening to you. You have no way to know what kind of impact your testimony—however modest it may be—will have on the life of another individual, or in turn, how that individual might use his own testimony to change the lives of still others.

By spreading the Word of God through the story of Jesus, we work to *preserve* life, peace and prosperity in our world.

CHAPTER 9

Christians as a Disinfectant

Rev. George Whitefield might have been the most extraordinary itinerant preacher in America in the eighteenth century. Whitefield, a native of England, began as an actor in his youth but, for whatever reason, ended up at Pembroke College, University of Oxford. Though Whitefield was eventually ordained a deacon in the Anglican church, while at Pembroke he made the acquaintance of, and spent substantial time with, John and Charles Wesley as part of their Christian students' club, which they called "the Holy Club."

Between his acting experience and his God-given gifts as a communicator, Whitefield was a most remarkable preacher. He was not at all dry, matter-of-fact, or monotone in his delivery, which was the standard order for preachers of his day. Instead, his methods were, well, unconventional. He cried; he danced; he screamed. His sermons were punctuated with tonal modulation, accents and emphasis in such a way that one could not help but be taken in by his teachings. He was, by today's standards, a walking PowerPoint presentation. He was quite skilled at whipping up the emotions of his listeners. David Garrick, a prominent British actor of the time, is reported to have said, "I would give a hundred guineas if I could say 'Oh' like Mr. Whitefield."

People loved him, despite his common reference to them in his sermons as beasts and devils. He was not welcome in America's colonial churches, not only because of his unusual style, but also because of his attacks on the organized religious institutions of the day. The stuffed-shirt traditionalists were unimpressed by his wild antics. Because of that, as he preached his way through the colonies in the mid-1700s, he did so in farm fields and on town-hall steps.

He drew huge crowds from all denominations. It was not uncommon for him to speak to thousands of people at a time. His preaching style held them spellbound and he brought the Bible to life in a way no one had ever seen before. As such, the masses hung on his every word. They felt connected to him because he had no script in front of him and no pulpit separating him from the throngs. Historian Murray N. Rothbard credits Whitefield as the person whose preaching sparked the Great Awakening in America (Murray N. Rothbard, *Conceived in Liberty, Vol. II* [Arlington House Publishers, 1975], pp. 160-61).

Whitefield arrived in Philadelphia in 1739 as the first stop on his two-year preaching whirlwind through the colonies. Benjamin Franklin, who eventually became lifelong friends with Whitefield, wrote that his preaching had an "extraordinary influence" on his listeners. Franklin wrote of Whitefield in his autobiography, specifically expressing the effect his teaching had on the people. Franklin said:

It was wonderful to see the change soon made in the manners of our inhabitants [of Philadelphia]; from being thoughtless or indifferent about Religion, it seemed as if all the World were growing Religious; so that one could not walk through the Town in an evening without hearing Psalms sung in different families of every street. (*Autobiography of Benjamin Franklin,* The Easton Press, 100 Greatest Books Ever Written, 1976, p. 137)

While it may be true that Whitefield's captivating style played a role, ultimately it was the Word of God that changed the hearts, and thus the manners, of the people of Philadelphia. God's Word disinfected their callous hearts and attitudes. In turn, it was the Word of God that lit the fires of the Great Awakening.

Whitefield did something even more remarkable for the times: he preached to slaves. He sought out slave audiences and wrote on their behalf. How he was able to accomplish this is unknown, except that the hand of God made it happen. Regardless, he had a profound effect on the lives of African slaves. *Christianity Today* reports that the slave response to Whitefield was so substantial that "some historians date it as the genesis of African-American Christianity" (http://www.christianitytoday.com/history/people/evangelistsandapologists/george-whitefield.html).

In the process of disinfecting the hearts of individuals, God's Word in turn disinfects society. There is no better example than that of slavery itself. Slavery was a burning issue in America since the importation of African slaves to the colonies began in earnest in the latter half of the seventeenth century. By 1700, leading pastors from all Christian denominations were speaking out against slavery and demanding the abolition of the abhorrent practice. Christian Quakers in Pennsylvania began denouncing slavery in the 1680s. By 1693, the Quaker church was taking official positions against slavery, beginning with criticizing the further importation of slaves (*Conceived in Liberty, Vol II*, p. 174).

One essay that was broadly circulated and widely read in the northern states in the early eighteenth century was a paper published in Boston in 1700 titled "The Selling of Joseph." In it, Massachusetts Judge Samuel Sewall made a compelling case against slavery, arguing that all people "have equal rights to liberty." Sewall used the Old and New Testaments as the exclusive legal authority for his positions (see "The Selling of Joseph," http://www.pbs.org/wgbh/aia/part1/1h301t.html).

Citing Leviticus 25:39 and Jeremiah 34:8-20 (among many other scriptures), Sewall pointed out that God's people "were strictly forbidden from the buying or selling of one another for Slaves." He argued that all sons of Adam "have equal rights to liberty."

The Quakers pressed hard through their congregations in the north for the abolition of not just the importation of slaves, but also the pracice of slavery in general. The Quakers expressed the well-rooted belief held by Americans (and later expressed in the Declaration of Independence) that natural human rights existed apart from civil government. The right under natural law to life and liberty extended to every human being. Based on both of these scriptural philosophies, the Quakers were successful in peacefully and voluntarily abolishing the practice of slavery in Pennsylvania and New York well before the first shots were fired in the war with England (never mind the Civil War)(*Conceived in Liberty*, Vol I, pp. 175-180).

When we think of why the colonies broke ties with England in the first place, the one thing that comes to just about everybody's mind is that the colonists objected to the idea of "taxation without representation." While that was one of the allegations of injustice by the king presented in the Declaration of Independence, which injustices the founders referred to as "repeated Injuries and Usurpations," it most certainly is not the only one. Indeed, *it is not even in the top ten* of the charges leveled against the Crown.

There are twenty-seven separate charges of abuse by the Crown cited in the Declaration of Independence. The Declaration states that these twenty-seven abuses have as their direct object "the establishment of an absolute Tyranny over these States." The allegation regarding taxation without representation is *seventeenth* on the list.

The number one item on the list of oppressive acts reads: "He [the king] has refused his Assent to Laws, the most wholesome and necessary for the public Good." This is a reference to the king's act of regularly vetoing various laws passed by the colonies, most notably the various legislation passed by the northern states to *outlaw* slavery (see *Elliot's Debates, The Debates in the Several State Conventions on the Adoption of the Federal Constitution*, Vol. II [U.S. Congress, 1836], p. 335).

Indeed, Benjamin Franklin, citing the action of Pennsylvania Quakers in freeing their slaves and abolishing the practice altogether, pointed out that a "disposition to abolish slavery prevails in North America." Franklin also pointed out that Virginia petitioned the king for a law to end the importation of slaves into Virginia but acknowledged that it would not likely be affirmed because "their former laws of that kind have always been repealed" (David Barton, *Original Intent, 5th Ed.*[Aledo, TX: Wall Builders, 2013], pp. 295-296).

After the colonies declared independence from England, just about all of them in the north quickly passed laws abolishing slavery. This occurred even before the U.S. Constitution was ratified in 1789. The Congress of the Confederation passed the Northwest Ordinance in July 1787 creating a new territory of the United States. Article VI of the Northwest Ordinance reads:

> There shall be neither slavery nor involuntary servitude in the said territory, otherwise than in the punishment of crimes, whereof the party shall have been duly convicted.

The Congress of the United States reenacted this law wordforword in 1789 after the ratification of the Constitution. As a result of this act, the states of Ohio, Michigan, Indiana, Illinois, and Wisconsin were admitted into the Union as non-slave states.

The fact is, virtually all the founders—the overwhelming majority of whom were Christians (as discussed below)—shared a general disposition for abolishing slavery. They knew that slavery was profoundly inconsistent with the language and spirit of the Declaration of Independence which rightfully states that "all Men are created equal, that they are endowed by their Creator with certain inalienable Rights, that among these are Life, Liberty, and the Pursuit of Happiness."

However, slavery was heavily ingrained in America by 1787, especially in the south, as it was an institution existing on this continent for over 150 years by that time. It was not the American founders who established slavery in America, nor was it the founders who sanctioned it. Rather, slavery was a product specifically of the Dutch and British governments' trading for many decades with African warlords whose captured prisoners of war were sold in slave markets around the world.

By contrast, Christians in America worked to abolish slavery—not just through the steps mentioned above, but also by pushing specific Constitutional provisions designed to end the grisly practice of importing slaves. Article I, Section 9 of the Constitution gave the Congress the power to *prohibit* the "Migration and Importation" of such persons whom the states saw fit to import. This provision is squarely pointed at the importation of slaves. The prohibition took effect beginning in 1808. In 1807, Congress passed a law banning the importation of slaves to America. President Jefferson signed the bill on the morning of January 1, 1808, the *very first day* he had the Constitutional authority to do so. That act forever ended the importation of slaves into the United States. Jefferson regarded the signing of that law as one of his greatest contributions to public life (Thomas Jefferson, *Writings: A Memorandum [Services to My Country]*,[NY: Literary Classics of the United States, 1984], p. 702).

Jefferson knew that slavery was immoral and repugnant and that it had to be abolished. He criticized it sharply in his writings and worked to abolish it while in public office at both the state and national levels. Jefferson, often branded an atheist, said this about the question of God's view of the matter:

And can the liberties of a nation be thought secure when we have removed their only firm basis—a conviction in the minds of the people that these liberties are the gift of God? That they are not to be violated but with this wrath? Indeed, I tremble for my country when I reflect that God is just: that his justice cannot sleep for ever: that considering numbers, nature and natural means only, a revolution of the wheel of fortune, an exchange of situation, is among possible events: that it may become probable by supernatural interference! (Jefferson, *Writings: Notes on the State of Virginia, Query XVIII*, p. 289)

Jefferson went on to say that "The *Almighty has no attribute* which can take the side" of a pro-slavery argument. Thus, Jefferson hoped "under the auspices of heaven, for the total emancipation" of all slaves in America (Jefferson, *Writings: Notes on the State of Virginia, Query XVIII*, p. 289, emphasis added).

Interesting comments indeed from one reputed to be an atheist.

America is often harshly criticized for allowing the practice of slavery in the first place. While the institution itself is indefensible, let us keep track of some very important facts. First, slavery was practiced everywhere in the world in the late sixteenth century, when slaves and indentured servants began finding their way into the new world. In fact, slavery is still practiced this very day in many Muslim nations throughout the world under Sharia law.

Second, of all the people of the world, America's Christian founders crafted the legal philosophy under which slavery was eventually abolished. That philosophy was expressed in the "equality" clause of the Declaration. During his political career, Abraham Lincoln referred to the Declaration's "equality" clause as the "crowning jewel" of American liberty. In his debates on slavery, he repeatedly pointed to Jefferson's words in the Declaration and God's word in the Bible as the moral and legal authority for abolishing slavery. That is exactly what happened, but only after Jefferson's worst fears were realized.

Third, we must recognize that America—through Christian men acting both in and out of government—abolished, first, the slave trade, and then, the institution of slavery entirely. Joseph Story was a Justice of the Supreme Court from 1811 until his death in 1845. Justice Story, a devout Christian himself, founded the Harvard University Law School and is the author of *Commentaries on the Constitution of the United States*. This extensive treatise on the historical and legal background and workings of the Constitution was required reading in law schools for generations. It is an epic work and is still considered the most authoritative narrative on the subject.

Justice Story addressed the question of the slave trade in his analysis of Article I, Section 9 of the Constitution. Regarding America's unique role in abolishing the slave trade, Justice Story observed:

> Let it be remembered that, at this period, this horrible traffic was carried on with the encouragement and support of every civilized nation of Europe; and by none with more eagerness and enterprise, than by the parent country [England]. America stood forth alone, uncheered and unaided, in stamping ignominy upon this traffic on the very face of her Constitution of government, although there were strong temptations of interest to draw her aside from the performance of this great moral duty. (Joseph Story, *Commentaries on the Constitution of the United States, Vol. II, Sec. 1334* [NJ: The Lawbook Exchange, Ltd,.], p. 193)

We should recall Justice Story's observation about America's role in crushing slavery:

> *It is to the honor of America*, that she should have set the first example of interdicting and abolishing the slave trade, in modern times (*Commentaries on the Constitution of the United States*, emphasis added).

It is interesting to note that Justice Story wrote the Supreme Court's opinion in the case of *United States v. Libellants and Claimants of the Schooner Amistad*, 40 U.S. 518 (1841) in 1841. The Supreme Court held that the unwilling passengers on board the *Amistad* were kidnapped Africans who were entitled to their freedom. That is the case that became the basis for Steven Spielberg's 1997 movie *The Amistad*.

God's Word was the dynamite that was planted under the structure of slavery—and it was put there, and the fuse was lit—by Christians determined to disinfect society. It is clear that by changing the hearts of individuals, those individuals can move to change the culture of their world for the better. We must act as disinfectant to the evils we see around us. It may be true that you can't change the entire world, but you most certainly can change your little corner of the world.

Indeed, the disinfecting qualities of Christianity are responsible for the most profound change the world has ever seen: the establishment of the United States and her Constitution. Until the founding of America, the governments of the world historically consisted of hereditary monarchies and tyrannical dictatorships. Governments were instituted or changed only through war, chance, revolution or conquest. America alone was founded as a republic based on the rule of law and not the whim of man. For the first time in human history, a government's founding documents expressly stated that the government's sole responsibility was to protect the natural rights of its citizens.

The legal systems of all governments are based on some kind of religious beliefs. Religion informs our individual morals, principals and behavior. It dictates how we raise our children and interact with our friends. It leads us in how we do our jobs and how we treat our co-workers. It shapes societal standards and, in the end, dictates the nature of the government under which we live. As I point out in chapter 4, George Washington, in his Farewell Address to the Nation in 1796, stated that religion and morality provide the essential foundation for the workings of good government. They are the two great pillars of political prosperity and individual happiness.

Christianity is the religion that shaped America. It alone provided the foundation for her political and social belief systems. De Tocqueville aw this very clearly and the Supreme Court's decision in the *Holy Trinity Church* case, which I discussed at length in chapter 3, recognized this as a matter of historical fact. Of the fifty-five delegates to the Constitutional Convention, 93 percent were members of Christian churches, including Episcopalians, Presbyterians, Congregationalists, Lutherans, Methodists, Catholics, and Dutch Reformed.

Various scholars and historians studied approximately 15,000 writings of the American founders, produced during the period from about 1760 through 1805. Researchers looked at letters, books, newspaper articles, pamphlets, etc. What emerged from that historical record is that the founders cited the Bible as the authority for their positions on civil government more than any other single source. Historian David Barton points out that the Bible accounted for "34 percent of the direct quotes in the political writings of the Founding Era." Barton concludes that indeed the Bible is our founding document (David Barton, *Original Intent*, pp. 231-232).

Behind the Bible in terms of influence on the thinking of the founders were the writings of three men. I discuss each of them in the order of the founders' reliance on their writings.

The first is Baron Charles Secondat de Montesquieu, a French jurist, professor, and legal philosopher. In 1748, he wrote the highly influential book titled *The Spirit of Laws*. He argued that the powers of government had to be divided so that absolute power would be not vested in one office. His authority for dividing the power of government into three branches—legislative, executive and judicial—flowed from Isaiah 33:22. He argued that society must be built on principals that do not change. In his analysis on the effect of religion on government, Montesquieu said:

The Christian religion, which ordains that men should love each other, would without a doubt have every nation blest with the best civil, the best political laws; because these, next to this religion, are the greatest good that men can give and receive. (Montesquieu, *The Spirit of Laws* [Great Books of the Western World, Book XXIV], p. 200)

The next most often quoted authority on civil law and government was William Blackstone. Blackstone was an English judge and law professor. He was perhaps the most prominent English jurist and preeminent legal scholar of the mid-eighteenth century. Between 1765 and 1769, Blackstone published his four-volume series on English law, titled *Commentaries on the Laws of England.* The treatise was wildly popular in the thirteen colonies. Indeed, despite the fact that the population of England was three times that of the colonies at the time, more copies of the *Commentaries* were sold in the colonies than in the Mother country (Brent Winters, *The Excellence of the Common Law* [The Armstrong & Winters Foundation Ltd., 2006], p. 234). Blackstone's work was the gold standard of legal reference material during the Founding Era, and indeed the series were standard text books for all American law students throughout the nineteenth century. Abraham Lincoln learned the law by reading Blackstone's *Commentaries.* Between 1787 and 1890, American judges cited Blackstone as authority for their legal positions more often than any other writer (*The Excellence of the Common Law*, p. 525).

Blackstone's central premise is that the Laws of Nature and the laws of Nature's God must control all the affairs of government. The concept is replete throughout his works and this had a major impact on the founders' thinking. In fact, for the opening clause of the Declaration of Independence, Jefferson borrowed from Blackstone's thinking when Jefferson wrote:

> When in the Course of human events, it becomes necessary for one people to dissolve the political bands which have connected them with another, and to assume among the powers of the earth, the separate and equal station to which the Laws of Nature and of Nature's God entitle them, a decent respect to the opinions of

mankind requires that they should declare the causes which impel them to the separation.

The third most quoted individual was John Locke. Locke was an English philosopher, theologian, and author. His two primary writings, released in 1690, are *Two Treatises on Civil Government*. In his discussion of the responsibilities of and limitations on civil government, he drew heavily from the Bible. In fact, Barton points out that in his first treatise, "he invoked the Bible in one thousand, three hundred and forty nine references" and "one hundred and fifty seven times" in his second treatise (*Original Intent*, p. 225).

Locke argued that a stable and successful government had to be built on what he called transcendent, unchanging principles. Locke said that the Law of Nature stands "as an eternal rule to all men, legislators as well as others. The rules that they make for other men's actions must be conformable to the Law of Nature, i.e., to the will of God" (*Two Treatises*, Book II, p. 285). He further pointed out that the laws of man must be made in accordance with and without any "contradiction to any positive law of Scripture, otherwise they are ill made" (*Two Treatises*, Book II, p. 285).

Very simply stated, the Law of Nature is God's law. God's law is binding on all creatures and it applies universally throughout the world. It applies to all people at all times. God's law is stable and acts to protect life, liberty and property. It is superior to all other law and human laws cannot contradict it. Blackstone referred to it as the "common law." He tells us from whence it comes:

The doctrines thus delivered we call the revealed or Divine law and they are to be found only in the holy scriptures. These precepts, when revealed, are found upon comparison to be really a part of the original law of nature as they tend in all their consequences to man's felicity.

Upon these two foundations, the law of nature and the law of revelation, depend all human laws; that is to say, no human laws should be suffered to contradict these. (*Commentaries on the Laws of England, Vol. I* [Legal Classics Library], p. 42)

The legal and political systems of America were thus built directly upon the premises of God's Word. As such, God's Word disinfected civil government of the poison of oppression in a way that never before occurred on the face of the planet. After America's founding, the plight of the average man improved more in the next two hundred years than it had in all the previous six thousand.

Look around you. Do you see anything that needs disinfecting? Apply the Word of God to the situation, as it is the most powerful of all disinfectants.

CHAPTER 10

Christians as Spice

As a professional tax litigator for over forty years, I have seen every kind of tax case you can imagine, and I've seen a few you can't. Over the course of that time, I worked with three people who won the lottery at some level. One person was awarded $100,000, and the other two awards were in the single-digit millions of dollars. So while no case involved a massive amount of money by today's lottery standards, at least in the case of the two who won several millions each, you'd think that such a windfall would be a positive, life-changing event. Not so.

Not only did winning the money not have positive effects, but also in each case it resulted in substantially negative effects. Indeed, all three people, none of whom knew any of the others, told me the same thing in just about exactly the same words: "The day I won that money turned out to be the worst day of my life."

In each case, the money led to family feuds, infighting, jealously and envy. Greed and selfishness surfaced and caused strife and anguish that tore the families apart. Long-lost friends and relatives came out of the woodwork looking for a handout or an investment in some "can't miss" business endeavor.

As a kind of ultimate crown of pain, each person had profound IRS problems, which is why they consulted me. In all cases, lottery winnings are taxable. The IRS wants its money despite the fact that, say, hypothetcally, your girlfriend absconded with your $100,000 winnings after persuading you to put the money into a joint back account, because, after all, what could go wrong?

All around us, people are chasing the riches of the world—money, homes, jewels, status, etc.—as a means of finding some level of personal fulfillment. They are, as it were, desperate for some spice in life. But if you're seeking fulfillment by chasing money and things, there will never be enough to satisfy you. You will be stuck in a hopeless cycle of chasing shiny objects that takes you nowhere and gets you nothing. Something will always be missing.

When there's no fulfillment in the pure joy of life, people look for it elsewhere. This is often what leads to substance abuse and self-destructive behavior. That pattern over time leads to addiction, whether it's drugs or alcohol, gambling, sex—whatever. It's amazing to me that in a country so rich with resources and opportunities, people are turning to mind-altering substances at a growing rate to seek some sort of gratification or escape.

According to the Centers for Disease Control and Prevention (CDC) the 2015 rate of drug overdose deaths in the United States was more than 2.5 times the 1999 rate. Adults aged 45–54 had the highest death rate from drug overdoses. Deaths from overdoses involving heroin tripled from 8 percent of total deaths in 2010, to 25 percent in 2015. Overdoses from just about every type of drug were up during that same period, including methamphetamine and cocaine. The increases apply to both males and females, and cover all age groups and ethnicities (CDC, *Drug Overdose Deaths in the United States, 1999–2015*, February 2017, Data Brief No 273, https://www.cdc.gov/nchs/data/databriefs/db273.pdf).

What are people missing in their lives that they seek gratification to the point of death from drugs that are well known to be dangerous and highly addictive?

While one may argue that many (or most) of these overdoses were accidental, one thing is for sure: suicide is not. Indeed, there is probably no greater measure of hopelessness than that one would take, or ever consider taking, one's own life. The CDC reports that in 2013, suicide was the tenth leading cause of death in America for all age groups. There were 41,149 suicides in 2013, which equates to 113 suicides each day (CDC, *Suicide: Facts at a Glance 2015*, https://www.cdc.gov/violenceprevention/pdf/suicide-datasheet-a.pdf).

To put this in perspective, a total of 58,220 U.S. service personnel died in Vietnam during the entirety of that war. During the Mid-East wars from September 11, 2001, through 2016, the U.S. lost a total of 8,704 military service men and women, and that includes non-combat related deaths. These deaths occurred in Operations Desert Shield, Desert Storm, Enduring Freedom (Afghanistan) and Iraqi Freedom (Iraq)(Congressional Research Service, *"American War and Military Operations Casualties: Lists and Statistics,"* 7-5700, April 26, 2017).

The emotional senses of being lost, worthless, hopeless, depressed, unwanted, unneeded, incapable, or guilt-ridden are not cured by the potions, pills or incantations offered by the world. And they certainly are not cured by money and objects. Only Christ the Savior can assuage the anguish of these often debilitating and sometimes overwhelming feelings. I point to the example of the blind beggar from Luke's Gospel (see Luke 18:35-42; also Matthew 20:29-43; Mark 10:46-52).

In verse 35, Jesus was on the road to Jericho when He encountered a blind beggar. As the excited crowd moved along, the blind man could hear the commotion. He asked what was happening. Someone told him that Jesus was passing by (see Luke 18:37). Upon hearing that, the blind man cried out, "Jesus, Son of David, have mercy on me" (Luke 18:38). This beggar knew who Jesus was. By acknowledging Him as the son of David, the man knew that Jesus was the Messiah, as that is a title for the Messiah given in Isaiah 11:1-3. While the man was blind, he could see that Jesus is Lord and Savior.

What is fascinating here was how the people around Jesus reacted to the blind man's plea. Those who were leading Jesus on His way tried to shut the beggar up. These were probably the local religious leaders, the hot-shot politicians and successful businesspeople. They told the beggar to be quiet (see Luke 18:39). They wanted to stop him from speaking with Jesus; they wanted to prevent him from getting close to or having any relationship with the person the beggar knew to be the Savior of the world.

This is exactly what the world does today. We see this everywhere, as God is pushed further out of sight and deeper into the recesses of private life. As I discussed in chapter 4, a relationship with Jesus is not just discouraged, it's criticized. This happens in our government agencies, with politicians, in public schools, with leaders of higher education, and in the media. The idea of Christianity is attacked as foolish and simplistic.

Yet what is amazing to me is not just what these people said to the beggar, but what they *didn't* say. Both in Luke's account of this story and in the world today, those who criticize the merits of a relationship with Christ *offer no alternative.* In the case of the blind beggar, those who told him to shut up didn't give him any other hope for curing his affliction. There was no plan of theirs he could follow to alleviate his plight or mitigate his suffering. They didn't offer healing, aid, treatment, comfort, or a job. They didn't even offer food, water or shelter to the destitute man. They just wanted him to sit there with his mouth shut and let Jesus pass by. As far as they were concerned, he could simply languish on the roadside in his poverty and hopelessness for the rest of his miserable life.

What the blind man did in response to the admonitions to shut up is the lesson in this. Rather than follow the directive to stay away from Jesus, verse 39 says that he shouted for Jesus all the more! He didn't let Jesus just pass him by. He called out over the objections of those who told him to keep his mouth shut. He didn't let anything stop him from getting close to the Savior.

Verse 40 tells us that Jesus heard his loud crying. How did He then respond to the man's continued prayers? Luke tells us that Jesus stopped nd ordered the man to be brought to Him. I like how Mark explains the man's reaction. Mark 10:50 says that he threw his cloak aside, jumped to his feet, and came to Jesus. Imagine the man's excitement upon realizing that his continued prayers got him face to face with the Savior, who in fact welcomed the poor lout to His side.

The man was brought to Jesus, who then asked what he wanted. Isn't that an odd question? Jesus could surely see the man was blind. He certainly knew the man was a beggar. He knew the man didn't have a 401(k) or medical coverage. He was destitute.

So why did Jesus ask the question? The man's attitude and response re the keys. They show that he confessed his sin. Luke 15:39 says that he man asked Jesus to have mercy on him. This shows submission to the ordship of Jesus. Then in verse 41, the man told the Lord, "I want to see."

The combination of the man's confession and submission brought God's blessing upon him. In verse 42, Jesus restored his sight, saying that he man's faith healed him. The crowd saw this and they all praised God.

When you introduce people to Christ, you offer them the greatest pice of life. You offer them the opportunity for the healing of all their fflictions—physical, spiritual and emotional. Jesus said that the thief omes to steal and destroy. But He came not only that we might have life, ut have it abundantly (see John 10:10).

My third child (second son), Nathan, is what psychologists would call "strong-willed child." That's psycho-babble to describe a child who does whatever he wants, whenever he wants. I call him the greatest challenge of my life. From the time he was six or seven years old, he was asserting himself at every level, marching to the beat of his own drum. Even at a very young age, before he had a command of English syntax, when I had o discipline him for some reason, he simply looked up at me and said, Leave-it me alone."

While he was a very intelligent child, he always had his own agenda. f my plans or demands, or those of his mother, happened to fit in, fine. If not, too bad. He was going to follow his own course regardless. And when Nathan made up his mind to do something, or *not* do something, there was no force on the planet that was going to disabuse him of the decision. I used to say to his mother that his mentality was such that he would lead thirteen divisions of combat troops across Europe someday.

As time went on, I came to be on a first-name basis with every principal of every school he ever attended. When my phone rang and I recognized that the call was coming from the school he happened to be attending, I answered by saying, "What happened this time?" It's not that he was a bad kid. There was never any criminal behavior involved—not that they could prove, anyway. In fact, Nathan loved the Lord and, even as a young teenager, spent a great deal of time working with my brother Mike in his ministry in the inner city of Minneapolis. It's just that he had his own plan and school work rarely was a part of it.

When he was about fourteen, I ran across an organization called the U.S. Navy Sea Cadets. It's a program that mimics the U.S. Navy experience. Think of it as Boy Scouts or Girl Scouts (girls participate equally) but based on the U.S. Navy's training environment. When kids join, they go through a mini boot camp. For Nathan, it was a two-week session that took place at the Navy's Great Lakes Naval Training Station in Illinois, just north of Chicago. The program is a micro-version of actual Navy boot camp, held at the very place where most naval recruits get their basic training. It's conducted by actual naval personnel. Though I expected to get a call about half way through telling me to come and get him, Nathan actually excelled in the program. In fact, he was named the honor cadet for his group of about seventy kids.

Early in his junior year of high school, as a result of yet another meeting with the principal and his guidance counselor, we decided that Nathan would leave that school. He would transfer to a local Army ROTC high school. The experience was very much like that of the Sea Cadets but instead of one or two weekends a month, and just one or two full weeks during the summer, this was daily emersion. Nathan responded very well to the discipline and structure. He excelled there too, moving up quickly through the student ranks. After about a year into this, Nathan announced to me that he wanted to join the military for real. He wanted to become a U.S. Marine.

I was a bit stunned: a Marine?

Thereafter, over the course of some time, I regularly talked with Nathan about this—not so much trying to dissuade him of the idea, but more so making sure he understood (1) the significance of the commitment he would have to make and (2) that he had options. And I was careful to impress upon him the options.

During one particular conversation in which I challenged the wisdom of this move, he said to me, "Dad, didn't you always tell us that we are to be servants? Didn't you tell us to have a servant's heart? Didn't you teach us that we have to serve others? Didn't you say, to whom much is given, from him much is expected? Isn't that what you always said? Well that's what I'm doing!"

I replied, "Nathan, that's not what I meant. I wasn't taking about the Marines."

I went on. "The Marines go to every hot spot in the world. They are the tip of the spear. They're the first in and the last out—*every time*. Marines get shot at! I wasn't talking about the Marines. I was thinking more along the lines of being a crossing guard in the church parking lot. You could wear a blaze orange vest and carry that cool flashlight that looks like a light saber. That's what I meant. Not the Marines!"

As I pressed further, he looked at me and calmly said, "Dad, this is where God wants me."

What do you do with that?

Well, I did what any Christian father would do under the circumstances. I looked Nathan square in the eye and I said, "You're grounded, buster! You wanna march? You can march right up to that room!"

To show you how that worked out, Nathan celebrated his nineteenth birthday on the top of a mountain in southern California called "The Reaper." It's located on Camp Pendleton, the U.S. Marine Corps base just north of San Diego. You can probably imagine why they call it The Reaper. That was the very day he finished his basic training and was awarded his Eagle, Globe and Anchor pin, officially making him a United States Marine.

At one point prior to this, as the time was fast approaching for Nathan to ship out for boot camp, I mentioned, almost in passing, that it was a good time for him to dial up his prayer life—to press in to God a bit closer, to dial into the Holy Spirit for the strength of mind and body it would take to get through his training. In his typical strong-willed fashion, he said, "Dad, if I can't do this on my own, I have no business doing it."

I reminded him that God puts all of us in positions where we need to lean on Him. In fact, He wants that. He wants us to draw strength and courage from Him. I pointed to Moses and Gideon as examples. Nathan responded by saying, "This is different. This is the Marines."

But not long into boot camp, my brother Mike received a letter from Nathan. Here's part of what it said:

Life is rough here. It's long and stressful days but the nights aren't long enough. I keep my chin up tho, and I am doing a lot of praying. I am actually a prayer leader and it has really brought me closer to the Lord. I was actually wondering if you could do me a favor. I would like to get some verses that pertain to boot camp printed on some index cards and laminated so that they do not get wrecked. I don't have a lot of time to look thru my Bible to find verses to read during our prayer groups. I would really appreciate it.

So this kid who didn't think he needed prayer not only needed it, but he was also helping those around him to seek strength from the Lord. These were all young kids just like Nathan. They were all eighteen to twenty years of age, all away from home—some for the first time—and some didn't even have families to get letters from. They were all in the same boat together under the most challenging and frightful of circumstances they faced to that point in their lives. They were getting very little sleep and not enough to eat. Early on, the lack of sleep got so bad that many recruits fell asleep right on their feet. The unluckiest of them would physically fall down before waking up, so everyone tried to make sure the guy next to him didn't fall asleep.

The recruits were pushed to the point of physical, mental and emotional exhaustion. They were pushed to the absolute limits of human endurance, and then they were pushed even further. At one point Nathan wrote us a letter that said his back hurt, his feet hurt, his legs hurt; he missed his bed and pillow; his missed his brother; he missed the dog; he wanted his mommy. He wasn't in boot camp three weeks and knew that he was going to have to lean on God in a big way to get through it.

In the midst of all this, Nathan prayed with and for the kids in that prayer group. In those sessions, they could see his inner strength. While he was just as exhausted, just as sore, just as hungry, just as emotionally drained as they were, he had the inner strength to keep going and to encourage the others to keep going. The unchurched kids saw that strength too. They saw how it was lifting up those in the group. While they had no idea where it was coming from, they knew one thing: they wanted that strength—they needed that strength! Nathan introduced them to, among other scriptures, Isaiah 40:31, keenly apt under the circumstances:

But those who hope in the Lord will renew their strength.
They will soar on wings like eagles; they will run and not grow weary, they will walk and not be faint. (NIV)

When people are put under extreme duress and are at the end of their physical and emotional ropes, that's exactly when they most need to cry out to Jesus, just like the blind beggar did: "Jesus, son of David, have mercy on me." And that's exactly what some of those unchurched kids did. Nathan led four kids to Christ through his prayer group in boot camp.

When Nathan entered boot camp, the idea of evangelism was not simply a low priority; it wasn't a priority at all. Moreover, the kid who didn't think he needed God's help soon realized that he probably wasn't going to make it through *without* God's help. He also saw that those around him—a group of scared, exhausted, lonely and homesick kids—needed it too. He offered them the greatest spice in all of life. He introduced them to the idea that they could not only draw strength from the Holy Spirit, but that with a confession of faith like that of the blind beggar, they would no longer be separated from God for all eternity.

CHAPTER 11

Making Salt Work

In Matthew 5:13, Jesus asks an important question that should give pause to us all. He says, "But if the salt loses its saltiness, how can it be made salty again? It is no longer good for anything, except to be thrown out and trampled underfoot."

We have seen that salt is a marvelous preservative, disinfectant and spice. But to be effective—and there's no way around this—it must come into contact with that which it intends to preserve, heal or spice. That is, for Christians to have a positive impact in these areas, they must come into contact with and actively demonstrate God's love and Christ's saving grace to a rotting, ungodly and hopeless world.

Salt can't stop meat from decaying if it's never applied to the meat. It cannot cleanse a wound or add flavor to food if it's left in the jar. You simply have to interact with the unsaved to offer the benefits of Christ. If you don't, you are like salt that has lost is saltiness. This is exactly analogous to the guy who got hired for a new job but never showed up for work.

Jesus gives us a perfect picture of this in Matthew 13:3-9 (see also Mark 4:1-9; Luke 8:4-8). This portion of Scripture is known as the Parable of the Sower. This parable speaks directly to the condition of a person's heart as he hears and receives God's Word. The condition of your heart is what determines your capacity to be salt to those around you.

In the Parable of the Sower, Jesus talks about a farmer planting seed. He explains later in the chapter that the seed is the Word of God. As the Word, or seed, is spread, it falls upon the hearts of mankind. The hearts upon which the seeds fall are like soil, which appears in one of four different conditions. As we examine the four conditions of the heart, ask yourself, "Where do I fall on this list?"

1. Matthew 13:4 says that some seeds fell along the path and were eaten by birds.

A well-used path does not contain soft soil. It's usually very hard and may even be paved with crushed rocks. The soil is probably sun baked since most paths are out in the open. The soil is definitely never turned and it's not fertilized. Nothing of value grows on the path.

This describes the hardened heart of a very stubborn person. This person is well set in his ways and often ignores the advice and counsel of experienced friends. It is difficult, at best, for the Word of God to penetrate this heart. This person has difficulty growing spiritually and emotionally. He seldom learns anything new and thus rarely improves himself. As a result, he often makes the same mistakes repeatedly.

When you harden your heart, you can't learn and grow. It's a simple fact that the minute you think you know it all, you stop learning. It is unlikely that such a person can be a preservative, a disinfectant, or a spice to anybody around him.

The lesson here is that you must keep your heart soft. You must be open and willing to learn new things and to receive instruction and guidance, about God's Word at a minimum, but also about life very broadly and generally. The broader your knowledge of life in general and the Word in particular, the greater the likelihood you can see problems, perceive solutions, and work with others to solve problems. In that sense, the salt comes out of the jar.

2. Matthew 13:5-6 says that some seeds fell in rocky places where there was little soil. The seeds sprouted in the shallow soil, but when the sun hit them, they withered because they had no roots.

Plants in shallow soil with no roots cannot endure harsh sun and drought. Here we are talking about people who willingly jump into tasks and take on challenges but have little or no background, training or education needed to get them through the process. They are eager at first, but as soon as the pressure gets turned up in some way, they shrink from the task.

Just as often, it's a lack of maturity that holds these people back. In their naiveté, they don't realize that there will be hardships. They don't understand that even for Christians, life is not perfect, fair or just. When they see problems manifest around them, their lack of personal depth pushes them out of the game.

Jesus makes it clear that we all will face challenges in life. In Luke 6:46-49, He described two men, each of whom built a house. One man built his house on a rock while the other built his on sand. Jesus said that storms and floods hit both houses. Note that the man whose house was built on the solid foundation of God's Word was *not* immune from the storms and torrents. But his house survived the onslaught because it was built on the rock of God's Word. The house built on sand collapsed.

The lesson here is that we have to deepen our understanding of God's Word and of the ways of the world because storms *will* come. But when you have a solid foundation of God's Word that you can put into practice, you benefit not only yourself and your family but also those around you. When their storms come—which they will— you become a source of strength, courage and encouragement to them. Your unchurched friends will see that strength and courage and wonder where it comes from. They will want it too, much the way Nathan's comrades in boot camp sought out his source of strength and courage.

3. Matthew 13:7 says that some seeds fell among the thorns, which grew up and choked out the plants.

In this case, the problem is not a hard heart. The seeds take root in soft soil and sprout. Nor is the problem that the plants are shallow rooted, because they do in fact grow up. The problem here is that thorns and weeds are growing right alongside the good plants. The thorns and weeds rob the desirable plants of nutrients, sun and water. The good plants never mature, and therefore they never produce any fruit.

In this case, we're talking about the things that go on in our lives that we allow to choke out God's Word. Such things are different for different people. They might include chasing money, glory, fame, or some kind of personal gain. They could be emotional problems such as greed, envy, selfishness, or any form of hedonism. It could be a lack of attention to family or a half-hearted performance at work.

In some cases the weeds are even more dangerous. Such things could include too much drinking, chemical abuse, gambling, or sexual immorality of any description. They might even involve deceitfulness, fraud, or criminal behavior at some level. The list of such possibilities is endless.

All of these things are like garden weeds. They grow up around the good plants and choke off the water, light and nutrients. They do this by taking your time, attention, energy and resources away from your walk with God. The promised fruit from God's seed never materializes. There is some measure of spiritual life but it becomes a mere formality. You go through the motions but there are no results.

We all have such weeds to one extent or another. The reality is, just like with any garden, you have to regularly and systematically pull out the weeds. And it's an ongoing process. You don't weed a garden once a year. Just when you think you have them all, another one pops up somewhere else. This is a source of frustration for many young Christians. Many believe that just by making a confession of Christ as Savior all unhealthy or ungodly thoughts, desires and behaviors will magically disappear. They don't. It's true you become a new creature in Christ, but you are still a human being with all the faults and failures that come with that title.

You have to weed your garden and you have to do it regularly. You have to keep the weeds down so that God's plants mature and produce fruit. In this way, you can be salt to those around you.

4. Matthew 13:8 describes the fourth and final condition of the heart. here Jesus says that some seeds fell on good soil and produced a crop.

This situation is the opposite of the other three. The heart is soft, so he Word takes root and the roots grow deep. As the plants mature, they re able to stand up to both heat and drought, conditions we know will rise from time to time. As time goes on, bad seeds and weeds are removed so that the good plants are not choked out.

The result is that this person produces fruit. Matthew says that the rop production maybe a hundred or sixty or thirty times what was sown. n any case, there is a crop. And it is very significant that Jesus does not ay that a specific amount of production must be realized. He does not riticize those who produce less fruit or somehow set apart those who roduce more fruit.

This is exactly the same message in the parable of the loaned money n Matthew 25:14-30. In that lesson we are told that the master, upon eaving on a journey, entrusted certain resources to this servants. To one ervant he gave five bags of gold. To another he gave two bags of gold. And to another servant he gave one bag of gold. Verse 15 says that he gave o each in accordance with his ability.

In time, the master returned and demanded an accounting. The servants with five bags and two bags each doubled what the master gave hem. To both of them—equally, and without qualification—the master aid, "Well done, good and faithful servant" (Matthew 25:21,23).

But the third servant buried the bag of gold he was given. He was fraid to lose the resources entrusted to him, so he did nothing. It was he vho incurred the master's ire. He was cast out. But notably, there was no distinction of award between the other two.

God has given all of us unique gifts and talents. He expects us to use hem to produce fruit for His glory and for the growth of His kingdom. When we produce fruit, we please God. It doesn't matter how much we roduce.

On the other hand, when we don't use our gifts to produce fruit, have some explaining to do. It's like the guy who got hired for the new but didn't show up for work. Even if you are the smartest, best educated most experienced person in your company, if you don't show up for wc it doesn't matter. No one cares. You can't help anybody solve problems grow the company if you are not there.

But even if you are not the smartest, or the best educated, or the m experienced person in your company, none of that matters if you are hardest worker. When you stand ready and willing to help solve ev problem, and you do your best on a daily basis to grow your compa with a servant's heart, you overcome all the other shortcomings.

This is how the salt comes out of the jar to become a preservative disinfectant, and a spice in your corner of the world.

CHAPTER 12

What Is Light?

In Matthew 5:14, Jesus says, "You are the light of the world."

Scientists, philosophers and theologians have been studying and defining light for thousands of years. Thinkers, including Aristotle, Augustine, Aquinas, Dionysius, and others, have written volumes on this simple question. I will not do the same thing here, trust me. I, however, point to two essential elements of light.

The first is to identify light as an object, that is to say, "light" as a noun. You can think of this in terms of the lamp on your end table you use to read at night, or the overhead fixture in your kitchen. Each of these things provides illumination. Illumination is the second element of light. It is this element that I focus on here. That is, "light" as a verb, the *action* of illuminating the darkness.

On the very first day, God created light (see Genesis 1:3). Before He did that, darkness hovered over the entire earth (see Genesis 1:2). Light drove out the darkness. In this sense, God provided illumination, allowing us to see everything around us. Light pierces the darkness. Illumination reveals the form and substance of all things. Likewise, light reveals behavior, whether good or bad.

Illumination in a more philosophical sense implies the concept of learning. That which "comes to light" is something that is learned, discovered or understood. Over time, facts can "come to light." A fact is a historical event, something that occurred or was said at a particular point in time. Facts are often hidden for a great number of reasons. When the are discovered or disclosed, it is said that they are "brought to light."

In the context of our current existence, light shows the way. It illu minates road signs and signals. It points out the twists and turns in th road. Light identifies danger of all kinds, including potholes, detours an wrong turns. It shows us the entrance ramps, lanes and exits on the vari ous roads of life so that we can get exactly where we need to go as quickl and safely as possible.

John 1:4-5 says that Jesus is the light of all mankind, that His ligh shines in the darkness, and that the darkness cannot overcome His ligh The darkness referred to here is a fallen and sinful world, overcome wit greed, evil, and injustice—all manner of human faults and failures. Th light is the light of life offered through the blood of Christ that wash away that sin. The sin and darkness of the world cannot overcome the li and light of Christ. In this way, Jesus drives out sin and darkness from th culture. When the light of Christ is made to shine on sin and evil, they a exterminated, as the darkness cannot overcome the light.

Let me illustrate this with the well-known story of Jesus and the d monic, from Matthew 8:28-34, Mark 5:1-20 and Luke 8:26-39. In Luke we learn that Jesus traveled east across the Sea of Galilee—into Genti land. We know it was Gentile land because Mark 5:13 tells us there we 2,000 pigs in the area where Jesus landed. Jews would not have been her ing pigs, as the animals were considered unclean. Rather, the Palestini people raised the pigs and sold the pork to the Roman army, which occ pied the area. Italian guys like sausage.

With His first step off the boat, Jesus met a man possessed. Jesus ask his name, and the man said, "Legion," because many demons possess him (see Luke 8:30). The man was clearly out of his mind. He was nak He couldn't be restrained. He lived in the tombs among the dead. He w fierce, as no person could restrain him. He would bruise himself wi stones and Mark said he would howl at night like an animal. In every w this man represents the condition of godlessness that exists all around us today.

One might ask, "What the heck was this guy's problem?" Well, he didn't have *a* problem; he had many problems—and they manifested themselves in five different ways.

1. He had no regard for social order. He was naked and lived in the tombs. He howled day and night, terrorizing the people around him. He must have been filthy as his living conditions were filthy.
2. He had no regard for his own personal welfare. He beat his own body with stones, inflicting all manner of bodily harm. Luke 8:29 says that he was shackled yet he broke the chains. Imagine the effect that had on his body.
3. He had no regard for law or government. He broke the shackles that were placed on him. He refused to submit or be restrained. The people made efforts to subdue him but they could not. He fought all authority.
4. He had no regard for other people. He tormented the countryside with his howling that went on day and night. Matthew says that he was fierce. He was physically threatening and violent to the people around him.
5. His life was not his own. He was totally under the control of this legion of demons. Luke 8:29 says that the demons would drive him into the wilds. It is clear from this that the man was a total slave to sin and darkness.

Luke and the other Gospel writers describe a terrifying picture of a person's life without Christ. Such a life is in total chaos. The darkness of sin and the culture of death that enveloped this man's life spilled over to the people around him. The Gospel writers perfectly describe the cancer that infects society when the light of Christ is hidden from the culture.

Without that light, individual lives degenerate. They degenerate s
cially, personally, emotionally, physically and legally. They degenerate
the point where people in this condition have no control over themselve
Rather, they are controlled by the ungodly forces of the world that wo
day and night to upset God's intended order of peace and prosperity. Th
are controlled by sin of every description.

On the other hand, Jesus has authority over all those forces. His lig
has unstoppable power over the forces of darkness. In Luke 8:28 we lea
that Jesus commanded the demons to come out of the man. At that poi
the man threw himself at Jesus' feet. Speaking through the man, the d
mons recognized that Jesus was the Son of the Most High God.

Think about this. Whereas the demons tormented the man insuffe
ably to the point of depriving him of any kind of meaningful life, th
clearly recognized that Jesus had absolute power over them. Verse 31 sa
that they begged Jesus repeatedly not to order them into the abyss. I
stead, the demons begged Jesus to let them go into the pigs, which I
allowed. The entire herd of pigs, thus inhabited by the demons, ran dov
a steep hill into the lake and drowned.

When the townspeople heard about this, they came out to see wh
happened. They found the demoniac sitting at Jesus' feet, much the w
a disciple would be. Luke 8:35 says that he was dressed and in his rig
mind. As Jesus was set to leave, the former demoniac begged to con
along with Jesus. Instead, Jesus told him to return to his home and t
everyone what God did for him. And that's exactly what the man did (s
Luke 8:39). He became a witness to the power of Jesus over sin and evil

So let's take a concise "before and after" look at the demoniac:

- Before Christ, he was out of control—after, he sat at the feet of Jesus.
- Before Christ, he was unclothed—after, he was clothed.
- Before Christ, he was out of his mind—after, he was in his right min
- Before Christ, he was possessed—after, he was healed.

- Before Christ, he had many demons—after, he was known as "the man from whom the demons had gone" (Luke 8:38).
- Before Christ, he lived among the tombs (a picture of death)—after, Jesus told him, "Return to your home" (a picture of life; Luke 8:39).
- Before Christ, he was a wild man—after, he was a witness to God's healing power.

As a witness for Jesus, we can imagine that the man's story was told far and wide, impacting a great number of people within his sphere of influence. This is yet another remarkable quality of light. It is indifferent to direction. In its natural state, light illuminates everything around it without discrimination. For example, when you light a candle, the light illuminates everything in the room.

Thus it is with the light of Christ. It drives out darkness across its sphere of reach. It drives out chaos, anguish, despair, self-destruction and disorder. In their place, we see the restoration of social order, hope, peace and prosperity.

Just like the demoniac, we have been saved from sin and despair. Perhaps your personal salvation story is not so graphic as that of the demoniac, but it is just as real and just as powerful. And like the demoniac, you are called to tell those around you what God has done for you. In that way, you are the light of the world.

CHAPTER 13

Christians as Light

In Matthew 5:14, Jesus said, "A city on a hill cannot be hidden."

We know from Matthew 5:14 that Jesus called us to be the light of the world. To me, this is a most incredible statement. It is remarkable because, in John 8:12, He says, "I am the light of the world." Think about this. Jesus is making a direct comparison between Himself and His followers. He is saying in clear terms that we are the hands and feet of Christ on Earth. Some might think that the "hands and feet" analogy is a trite Sunday school colloquialism. However, the fact that Jesus used the same powerful words to describe His followers as He used to describe Himself tells me that this is something we better pay close attention to.

As a Christian, you and your story become Christ's light to the world. And just as salt must be mixed directly into an object if it's going to preserve, disinfect and spice that object, so too your light must shine in the *darkness* to be seen. That is, you must work to illuminate danger, to point out road signs, potholes, wrong turns, and yes, sin, in a dark and fallen world. As the light of Christ, you are called to witness to those around you, just as the demoniac was told to do after his salvation.

In this sense, "light" is a verb, not a noun. It implies action. In Matthew 5:15, Jesus says that people do not light a lamp and put it under a basket. Rather, they put it on a table so that it provides light to the entire room. The notion that you are the light of the world implies that you are to provide illumination to a dark world. Even more pointedly, it's not enough to be a Christian on Sunday at church. In that sense, you are light in an already lit room. If that's all you ever did, it's as if you were walking around in broad daylight with a lighted flashlight in your hand. Who is helped by that? Imagine yourself walking through the church parking lot at 11 o'clock in the morning and you're met by a parking lot attendant with a flashlight. He shines the light on the curb so that you don't trip. How impressed by that act do you think you would be?

Similarily, a light hidden in a dark room is worthless. It's like salt that lost its saltiness. Instead, the light of Christ shining through you must be put up high—to shine forth—so that all who are in the dark may benefit. Otherwise, the room remains dark.

In not one but two separate statements, the late Ronald Reagan described America as a shining city on a hill. The first time he made the statement, he was governor of the State of California in 1974. The second time was in 1979, when he announced his candidacy for the presidency of the United States. As evidenced by the writings of de Tocqueville, which I discussed earlier, America held out hope to the world that people could flee oppression and find liberty through her unique form of government based solely on Christian principals. Indeed, for many generations, Christian America was that shining city on a hill. Unfortunately, the light is going out. America is losing the culture war because her people are no longer light to a dark world.

It's time to reverse that trend, and the story of Jesus and the demoniac gives us instruction on how to do just that.

1. Jesus reached out to the demoniac right where he was. The demoniac lived across the Sea of Galilee deep in Gentile land. Jesus was far away from Jewish culture and Mosaic Law. Even worse, the demoniac lived in the tombs. This was the very symbol of death. In fact, in the Jewish culture, dead bodies were unclean. Tombs were unclean. No Jewish religious leader would have ventured into the tombs to meet with any individual who lived there.

Yet, Jesus went to the demoniac. He didn't ask or require the demoniac to come to Him. Luke illustrates this same point several times in his

Gospel. In Luke 7:1-9, a Roman centurion had a servant whom he valued highly. The servant was sick and about to die. Luke 7:6 says that Jesus, after meeting with certain individuals the centurion sent to speak with Him, went to meet the centurion's servant. Note this: Jesus went to the sick servant.

In Luke 7:12-17, Luke tells us the story of the widow and her dead son. As Jesus was approaching the gate of the town of Nain, He and His party met a funeral procession leaving the town. The deceased was a young man who was being carried on the funeral pallet. The dead man was the only son of a widow. Thus, this woman lost not only her husband but her son was well.

Certainly, she was distraught and crying. Jesus saw this and approached her. He told her not to cry (see verse 13). Then He did something extraordinary, exactly analogous to meeting the demoniac in the tombs. He touched the stretcher on which the dead man was being carried. Again, Jesus defied religious norms by touching an unclean object in order to bring peace and healing to the afflicted. At this point, the procession stopped. Then Jesus said to the dead man, "Get up," which he did (see verses 14-15).

In Luke 8:40-56, we learn about the story of Jesus and the daughter of Jairus, a synagogue leader. Jairus's daughter was sick and dying, and Jairus pleaded with Jesus to come to his house to heal the girl (see verse 41). They set out to the home of Jairus. While Jesus was dealing with yet another crisis along the way (a bleeding woman), a man approached the group and told Jairus that it was too late. The girl was dead and Jesus should not waste His time (see verse 49). But Jesus went to the house anyway. He raised the girl from the dead (see verse 54).

These are critical lessons. We need to reach out to people—to shine our lights—where people are right now, in the condition in which they find themselves today. We cannot ask or expect them to change their behavior or alter their patterns *before* we reach out to them. We have to shine the light into the darkness of their distress, sin, despair and disarray in order that God's presence can change their hearts and lives. To wait until they have found Christ's saving grace is like shining our flashlight in broad daylight.

2. Jesus didn't wait for the "right time." Jesus sailed across the Sea of Galilee with some of His disciples to the land of the demoniac. As they sailed, a storm came up and threatened to swamp the boat (see Luke 8:22-23). While it was common for storms to arise suddenly on the Sea of Galilee, the expert fishermen with Jesus could probably have predicted, and Jesus Himself could well have known, that such an event would arise given the conditions of the day.

But He didn't wait for the "right time." He knew the demoniac was on the other side of the lake and He knew the demoniac was in immediate distress; likewise the widow and her dead son, and the daughter of Jairus. When the opportunity presented itself, Jesus took full advantage then and there to demonstrate His healing power.

This lesson is clear: when the door of opportunity opens—regardless of the circumstances—you must walk through it to do what Christ would do. You must shine the light of grace, healing, peace, forgiveness and resurrection upon the situation. Don't succumb to the temptation to which we all fall victim, that "this is not the time or the place," that you will do it later when the circumstances are better. For any number of reasons, there may not be a next time.

3. Jesus got out of His comfort zone. The idea of (1) crossing the Sea of Galilee in questionable weather, (2) continuing across in the teeth of a storm, (3) meeting a possessed man living as a social outcast among the tombs of the dead, and (4) being in a land inhabited by unbelievers herding thousands of unclean animals, was way, Way, WAY out of the comfort zone of any Jew, especially those of the religious establishment. No traditional Jewish rabbi of the time would ever have done such a thing under any circumstances.

Of course, Jesus was no traditional Jewish rabbi by any stretch. He was the Son of God. He was not constrained by religious norms and neither should we be. He did things differently and boldly, and so too should we. He was concerned only with the salvation of His people, and so too should we. He worked always to ease their pain and suffering, and so too should we. We have to get out of our comfort zones to do this.

Without a doubt, my son Nathan was way out of his comfort zone in boot camp. At one point, he started getting flack from a drill instructor about his time at church and in prayer group with the other recruits. The reason is that Nathan and his friend Matt (whom I talk more about later) were assisting the Navy Chaplain with the Sunday morning church service. To do that, they had to leave the platoon squad room about a half hour before church and return about a half hour after the service ended. As the time approached for boot camp to come to an end, the platoon was focused on "final drill," the competition to determine the best training platoon of the thirteen-week session. The recruits attended to thousands of details surrounding their uniforms, their weapons, Marine Corps history, and on and on, in meticulous fashion.

As Nathan and Matt prepared to leave the squad room one Sunday morning, they were verbally accosted by a drill instructor. They were accused of leaving, not for church purposes, but to get out of the intense work leading up to final drill. The drill instructor publicly announced that the two were leaving because they were going to the Chaplain's office to hang out and eat candy. You can imagine that such news didn't go over too well with the other recruits.

Over the next three days, the drill instructor went on a verbal tirade against them. He was visibly angry and physically hostile. At one point he told Nathan that the Marine Corps had nothing to do with religion and that God had no place there. He claimed that God couldn't help Nathan in the face of what the instructor was going to dish out. Over the course of the several minutes-long diatribe, his voice grew louder and his tone more intense to the point where another instructor finally pulled him out of Nathan's face.

Boldly, Nathan pushed back. He took advantage of the so-called "Amnesty Box." This amounts to a complaint box in which a recruit may confidentially place a complaint card about a drill instructor who stepped over the line in some way during training. The complaint goes only to the senior drill instructor who then has the sole discretion to deal with it accordingly. Nathan complained not so much about the treatment to which he was subjected, but the statement that God has no place in the Marines and Nathan should keep his religion to himself.

The senior drill instructor questioned Nathan about the facts. Nathan explained the situation and called into question how it could be that God has no place in the Marine Corps, when it was God's leading that brought him there in the first place. The senior drill instructor assured Nathan that the offending instructor was out of line, and that of course God had a very important place in the Marine Corps. As a result, the instructor was taken out of service for a couple of days, and Nathan and Matt were never again harassed about their work for the Chaplain and the prayer group.

Nathan was in a situation in which he had no power and no leverage. He was an eighteen-year-old recruit in Marine Corps boot camp. Despite this, he didn't let the taunts, rants and physical intimidation of one man, as powerful as he was under the circumstances, keep him from talking about God.

4. To Jesus, every soul is precious. To me, this element is the most fascinating part of the story. Look at this picture: Jesus made a very dangerous trip across the Sea of Galilee through an intense storm. He did what no Jewish rabbi or religious leader of His day would have done, that is, go into a graveyard to meet with a demon-possessed man.

For what? It is obvious that Jesus went after just *one man*. We know this because as soon as He cast the demons out of the man, just when the man was restored to normal, Jesus left. He sailed back across the lake to

His home. This makes it clear that in the eyes of Jesus, every soul is precious. He cares about everybody.

This is entirely consistent with three great stories, all presented in the fifteenth chapter of Luke's Gospel. They are the stories of the lost sheep, the lost coin, and the lost son. We know the story of the lost son as the prodigal son. In each case, something of great value was lost. In the case of the sheep, Jesus posed a hypothetical situation involving a person who owned one hundred sheep but one of them was lost. Jesus pointed out that the shepherd would leave the other ninety-nine sheep to look for the lone lost sheep. And when he found it, he would call his friends in joy, announcing that he found his lost sheep (see Luke 15:3-7). Using the same analogy in Matthew 18, Jesus adds to the teaching by saying that the shepherd would be happier about finding the one sheep that wandered off than he would be about the ninety-nine that did not (see Matthew 18:12-14).

The story of the lost coin is a similar hypothetical situation in which Jesus described a woman with ten silver coins who lost one. She lit a lamp and swept the entire house, searching carefully until she found it. And when she did, she likewise called her friends in joy and announced that she found the lost coin (see Luke 15:8-10).

The story of the prodigal son is a discussion of a boy who left the care and nurturing of his father's estate to venture into a lost and dark world. He blew his money and found himself hopelessly mired in poverty. When he finally came to his senses, he returned home to his father's love. The story is a magnificent picture of sin, confession, forgiveness and restoration. Luke 15:20 says that the boy made a decision to return to his father and headed home. Then we learn that while the boy was "still a long way off, his father saw him and was filled with compassion." How is it that the father could see his son coming while he was still a long way off? He saw his son because *he was looking for him* (see Luke 15:11-27).

We need to keep this in mind when dealing with our friends and neighbors. How many times have you said or thought that so-and-so is a lost cause? "There's no hope for X." Sometimes maybe you reach such a level of frustration that you don't even want to open your mouth another time. But compare your "lost cause" with the condition of the demoniac, for example. I'm sure all the townspeople looked at him as a colossal lost cause. How much worse could his condition have been? And yet Jesus defied religious norms and all human common sense to reach out to the man right where he lived—directly and personally in his lost and miserable condition. The one and only thing Jesus asked for in return was that the man should tell everybody in the town what God did for him (see Luke 8:39).

We aren't responsible to "save" people, not in the physical sense, and most certainly not in the spiritual sense. Only God can do that. Thus, the outcome of our witness is, quite frankly, not our problem. It's God's problem. The Holy Spirit alone softens hearts and opens minds. All we can do is exactly what Jesus told the demoniac to do: tell others how much God has done for us.

CHAPTER 14

Do It for the Glory of God

I found out much of what I know about Nathan's boot camp experiences not from Nathan but from his friend Matt. Matt was in Nathan's platoon. He is a Christian kid from south Texas, about Nathan's age. He is now married and has a young family. When Nathan was home on leave after completing his training, he and I and some friends were sitting by the lake talking and carrying on. Nathan got a phone call from Matt. After a few minutes, I heard Nathan say, "I want to introduce you to my dad, Dan." Then he handed me the phone. "Dad," he said, "you'll like this kid."

Matt and I talked for some time. He told me he helped Nathan with the prayer group but that Nathan was the solid leader the other kids needed and looked to for spiritual strength. He told me that Nathan led four kids to Christ during those prayer sessions. Nathan never told me that. Later I asked him why he didn't tell me the story. He said, "It was no big deal, Dad. It wasn't about me."

He was only half right. It *wasn't* about him. But it *was* a big deal.

When you live out your Christian walk on a daily basis, the world around you sees that light. This is just what God wants. Matthew 5:16 says, "In the same way, let your light shine before others, that they may see your good deeds." Your Christian walk provides an example to a dark world. Your words and actions identify danger, evil, potholes, wrong turns, sin and injustice. You become an example for others to follow so that they avoid problems. By doing so, the world around you becomes a better place through the redeeming, transforming power of God. This is

he essence and core of evangelism, and given the direction the world is
going in general, and our nation in particular, it's never been more important to be that example.

By telling us to be salt and light, Jesus is telling us to function as a positive influence on our fellow man and, in the process, to show the blessings of God. In this process, salt operates internally while light operates
externally. Salt works by mixing directly with the people around us to
influence them at a personal level. Light works by broad illumination so
that everybody may see the love, forgiveness and salvation offered by God
through His Son.

Let's be clear on this important point: The conduct of good deeds
in your daily life is *not* for your glory. As Nathan said, "It's not about
me." Matthew 5:16 explains the purpose of good works, saying,"let your
light shine before others, that they may see your good deeds *and glorify
your Father in heaven*" (emphasis added). First Peter 2:12 reads, " Live
such good lives among the pagans that, though they accuse you of doing
wrong, they may see your good deeds and glorify God on the day he
visits us."

It couldn't be simpler. We are salt and light not for our own glory
but to glorify God. The world knows that actions always speak louder,
stronger and clearer than words ever do. The world knows well that talk is
cheap. People always take note of what you do—how you act—especially
if you profess to be a Christian. Do you live out what you claim to believe?
If you do, that's what people see and that's what they respond to. When
they see Christ in you, they want Him for themselves.

I don't pretend this is necessarily easy. In fact, it's generally not.
Christians are criticized, marginalized, and belittled. Nevertheless, we
have unique opportunities in America that too often we take for granted.
Despite the attack on Christianity, we still can worship freely. There's a
church on every corner. Bible studies meet everywhere and the government doesn't license religion or worship (yet). The Bible is widely avail-

able in any language. And we still have a First Amendment right to free speech.

Compare this with the conditions existent elsewhere in the world. In many places today, Christianity is outright illegal. Christians around the world are persecuted regularly. They are beaten and imprisoned. In Muslim countries, converting to and practicing our faith can get you killed.

The apostle Paul suffered through all of this, up to and including death. He gives us a glimpse of his sufferings for Christ in 2 Corinthians 11:23-29. There he explains that he:

- Spent time in prisons,
- Was flogged often,
- Was exposed to death time and again,
- Five times received 39 lashes from Jewish leaders (his own people),
- Three times was beaten with rods,
- Once was pelted with stones,
- Was shipwrecked three times,
- Spent a night and day adrift on the open sea,
- Was in danger both in cities and in the country,
- Was endangered by false believers,
- Went without food and sleep,
- Was cold and naked, and
- Was constantly on the move, in danger from rivers, from bandits and even from his fellow Jews.

And as if all of that was not bad enough, he explained that he daily faced the pressures of his ongoing concerns for the churches he planted throughout the region.

Now, friends, I'm sure you'll agree with me that there's not one of us who has to face anything close to what Paul experienced as a result of our testimony for Christ. Yet what Paul described here is the difference between dedication and commitment with respect to a given project. Let me illustrate using the example of a ham-and-egg breakfast. In a ham-and-egg breakfast, the chicken is dedicated but the pig is *committed*.

God has given each of us unique gifts to use for His glory. He's given us a unique platform, small though it may be, to talk about everything God has done for us. He's given most of us a ministry, however modest, through which to touch people with our gifts. So this begs the question, what is your personal attitude about the process? Are you dedicated or committed?

Sure, you might be criticized, belittled, called names, or made the butt of jokes. But that is nothing compared to what Paul lived through. Yet, most definitely, he was *committed* to his ministry. In 2 Corinthians 6:4-5, he summarizes in plain terms what he endured:

- Troubles, hardships and distresses,
- Beatings, imprisonments, and riots,
- Hard work, sleepless nights, and hunger.

But through it all, first and foremost—ahead of everything else (even his own life), Paul had as his top priority the need to talk about Jesus. And he traveled the known world doing so. By contrast, we can do it right where we live. And we can do it without fear of beatings, riots, imprisonment or stoning. We aren't going to be stranded at sea and we aren't going to be naked in the night while starving.

Regardless of the level of resistance and personal attacks you might be subjected to, never lose sight of God's promise in Matthew 5:10. There Jesus said that those who are persecuted and falsely accused of evil are in fact blessed because their reward in heaven is great. Moreover, the world doesn't persecute Christians because they necessarily hate Christians. They persecute Christians, the emissaries of God, because the world hates God. John makes this clear in John 3:19-21. Though Jesus came into the world as the light of the world, the world yet loved darkness. People love darkness because their deeds are evil and they believe that, in darkness, those deeds can be hidden from God. But the light of God exposes those dark deeds. That's what they fear and hate.

In 2 Corinthians 6:6-7, Paul explains how he was able to persevere through his persecution. He held firmly to:

- Purity, understanding, patience, and kindness,
- The Holy Spirit,
- Sincere love and truthful speech,
- The power of God, and
- The weapons of righteousness in both his hands.

Let's pay close attention to Paul's teachings as we apply this to our witness. We need…

Purity, because people are looking at you. As I said, and as everybody knows, actions speak louder than words and people will reject what you say if your actions contradict your words. Consistency in your Christian walk is a critical aspect of your testimony.

Understanding, because most people of the world are selfish and shortsighted. They want only what's best for them. Unfortunately, too often they don't even know what's best for them. We see this in politics at all levels. People no longer ask what's best for the country. They want to know what's in it for them. Even worse, jaded people always believe there's a self-serving angle to every good thing other people do. And while they probably cannot understand your sincere motivation as a Christian to talk about and live for the Lord for the sake of the greater good, you can understand their skepticism and address it.

Patience and kindness, because people of the world care only about themselves. It is very frustrating to deal with people whose only goal is to grab whatever handful of life's bounty they can, regardless of the pain or embarrassment it might cause others. But as Christians, we must have patience and show kindness to such people, despite their self-centeredness.

Love, because people respond when they believe that you truly care about them. It's fascinating to see their skepticism and cynicism melt away when, through love alone, you reach out to a hurting and lost person and make it known that you can and will help in his hour of need—with no strings attached. That's when you have the best opportunity to reach people with your words.

Truthful speech, because there's always power in truth. The truth sets people free. The truth dissolves the bonds of slavery. Always speak the truth to people—in kindness and love to be sure—but never hold back the truth.

With *the weapons of righteousness* in your right hand and left. Paul used the analogy of a Roman soldier, something every inhabitant of the Roman world could understand since the army was everywhere. A Roman soldier held a sword in one hand and a shield in the other. The sword was his primary weapon of attack and the shield his chief means of self-defense. In Ephesians 6:10-17, Paul tied this concept directly to his description of the armor of God. There he describes the tools with which we fight, including the belt of truth, the breastplate of righteousness, the shield of faith, the helmet of salvation, and the sword of the Spirit, which is the word of God. These are the tools with which we take on the world, and with which we testify about everything that God has done for us.

In all these, there are two very important tools to which Paul refers in both 2 Corinthians 6 and Ephesians 6. They are:

1. The word of God, which he calls the sword of the Spirit, and
2. The Holy Spirit, by which force we are able to dial directly into the power of God.

These are the ultimate weapons of attack and the means of self-defense that got Paul through all his tribulations and persecutions. These tools gave him the strength to be simply unbeatable in his faith and his work. They can give you that strength, too.

I need to be clear on another thing as we wrap up this discussion. You do *not* perform godly deeds to *become* a Christian. Your résumé does not get you hired. The shed blood of Jesus alone is the only way to restore your relationship with God and gain everlasting communion with God. Rather, you perform godly deeds *because* you are a Christian. But even at that, you do not do so for your own glory. Instead, you do so to show the world that the one true light of life is Jesus Christ.

CHAPTER 15

Who Gideon Was Not

In chapter 2 I talk about the idea of sharing the gospel message with friends and family. In fact, using the story of Gideon's first mission, I make the argument that it is with our own friends and family—those closest to us—that we should start. But we are often intimidated and reluctant to do so because of the potential social consequences of talking about religion and politics.

Yet, Gideon's first mission was to do exactly that. He was called by God to destroy the idols within his own family. He was to tear down his father's altar to the false god Baal and destroy the Asherah pole erected next to the altar. In their place, he was to build a proper altar on the very same spot and make a proper sacrifice to the living God on that very altar. The fire was to be built using the wood from the Asherah pole.

Can you imagine the dinner table conversation after Gideon did that?

I offer the story of Gideon's first mission to illustrate how we are to interact with our family when it comes to God's Word. That said, I know many people will respond by saying, "I'm no Gideon." I get it. Gideon was a biblical superstar. He is a character who is larger than life. Christian children study about Gideon and his army in Sunday school and learn how he led his ragtag band of three hundred soldiers against the powerful Midianites and literally chased them out of the land. You might wonder how you can ever live up to the standards of such a person.

This response is no doubt fully justified. That's why I think it's important to take a closer look at Gideon. We need to understand not only who he was but, more important, who he was *not*.

We know Gideon was chosen by God to free Israel from bondage. His ultimate mission was to destroy the Midianites and deliver Israel from the years of oppression to which they were subjected. The process began when an angel of God appeared to him out of the blue. The angel said, "The Lord is with you." The angel then tagged the statement with a very interesting phrase, and I think it's that phrase that causes everybody to believe that they cannot possibly fill Gideon's shoes.

In the NIV translation, the angel refers to Gideon as a "mighty warrior" (Judges 6:12). This tag has most certainly stuck with Gideon throughout time because that's exactly how we think of him.

This begs an important question and it weighs on me. It probably bothers you as you reflect on my challenge to follow Gideon's example. You see, I'm not a mighty warrior. I have no experience in such things. I don't know how to use the weapons of war. In fact, I am pretty certain that I couldn't function under the extreme stress brought on by the death and destruction that go along with war. I am likewise certain that I would be quite unable to make accurate life-and-death decisions in a split second with imperfect information in an environment of total chaos while under unimaginable duress.

I don't even believe it's a skill that one can learn really. Sure, you can go through training and gain some experience, but there has to be a great deal of instinct and intuition involved. I believe that most of us simply cannot do what true warriors do. That's probably one reason there are only 200,000 active-duty Marines in the U.S. They are the quintessential example of true warriors.

I'm not that, and you probably aren't either. So the weighty question is, where did Gideon learn to become a warrior?

For further context, let's take a closer look at Gideon's situation. The Israelites were captive to Midian. They were living under the harshest of subjugation. Their crops and livestock were stolen to the point that they were in deep poverty (see Judges 6:1-5). The fact seems to be that there were no warriors whatsoever among the Israelites at the time. Otherwise, how could all of that oppression continue over such a long time to the point where the Israelites cried out to God for relief (see Judges 6:6)? Certainly there was no man among them who could deliver them.

Gideon surely didn't classify himself as a "mighty warrior." Indeed, when the angel announced that Gideon was being tapped by God to lead Israel, he responded by saying, in essence, "You have the wrong guy." Gideon questioned how he could possibly lead Israel. He pointed out to the angel that he was the weakest member of the weakest clan (see Judges 6:15). That doesn't sound like a mighty warrior to me. In fact, at the risk of sounding crass, it seems like Gideon was a bit of wimp—*the weakest member of the weakest clan?*

Nor can we say that God made him into a warrior before He sent him out on his missions. Quite the opposite is true. God didn't change Gideon's character or personality before commissioning him. In Judges 6:14 we are told that God told Gideon that he was to "go in the strength you have and save Israel." It is clear that God didn't impart supernatural strength, courage, or wisdom to Gideon. As far as God was concerned, Gideon had all he needed to do the job (though he didn't know it at the time). Moreover, God promised Gideon that He was sending him (see Judges 6:14) just like He promised Moses.

The answer to the Gideon puzzle seems obvious to me—and normal people can take great comfort in this. Gideon *wasn't a warrior.* True, many translations use the phrase "mighty warrior;" however, both the King James and the RSV translations use the phrase "mighty man of valor." There is a very important difference between the two, and under the circumstances, the word "valor" is probably more accurate. Consider the context:

1. There is no history that Gideon was a warrior or a soldier of any kind before God tapped him. We have no evidence that he led—or was

even a party to—any kind of battle against the enemy. He wasn't even a civic leader among his people. He was, in every sense of the word, just a guy.

2. None of his family were warriors. Gideon himself described his entire clan, certainly to include his family, as weakest among all of Israel. As such, they had no background, skill, training, or experience in war such as could be passed on to Gideon in some way. Indeed, his father adopted the false idol worship of the Midianites. That seems to me to be the ultimate sign of surrender to one's oppressors.

3. Most significantly, Gideon was hiding from the Midianites. When God's angel found Gideon, he was buried in obscurity, grinding grain in a winepress to hide it from the enemy (see Judges 6:11). He wasn't leading scouting parties. He wasn't sabotaging enemy food supplies, or stealing weapons caches, or interrogating prisoners. He was hiding.

This does not describe a "mighty warrior."

On the other hand, the term "valor" is much different. It describes a person of courage and bravery. It describes a person with the commitment to do the right thing, even under great adversity. A person of valor forges ahead with a boldness of action. The Latin word for "valor"—*valere*—means to have value, to be of worth. In that context, Gideon most certainly measured up.

When God's angel told Gideon to go in his own strength, he wasn't talking about physical strength like that of a Roman soldier. He was talking about the courage, commitment, and boldness that God certainly detected in Gideon's personality. He was surely talking about the inner strength to follow God's call and to be obedient to Him in all circumstances. We are talking about the mental and emotional strength to surrender one's own will to God's will and to follow His plan unquestioningly.

That is the kind of person God is looking for to carry His word to the people. And that's exactly why God chose the weakest person from he weakest clan, precisely so that Gideon (and you) will rely entirely on God's power to carry the day.

God specifically did not choose a warrior in the sense that David, Sampson and the U.S. Marines are warriors. We know that God reduced Gideon's army to just three hundred men, who in turn moved against a far superior force. In doing so, He created a condition in which Gideon was totally reliant on God alone and most definitely had to remain so.

It is clear to me that God provided the supernatural power for Gideon's battle. Consider these facts: Gideon's army of three hundred men surrounded the Midian camp at night. Gideon's men didn't even carry the implements of war into battle; rather, they carried trumpets and clay jars with torches inside (see Judges 7:16). Those objects seem more suited to a parade than a battle. The men attacked in the middle of the night, breaking their jars to expose the light, while blowing their trumpets and shouting (see Judges 7:19-20).

The surprise, noise and sudden light scared the enemy to the point where they ended up turning their weapons on each other, and then they ran for their lives (see Judges 7:22). Now listen to this: Gideon's army won the day without even engaging the enemy in battle. Verse 21 says that each man in Gideon's army "held his ground" while the enemy panicked and ran.

How were they able to win this great victory without firing a shot and without losing a man? They did it through God's power, not Gideon's. He gave Gideon the courage and led him step by step through the process. He will do the same thing for you. God will provide the power and courage you need to carry out your mission.

We all have the same tendency that Gideon showed when tapped by God to carry out a mission. We believe that God made a mistake and picked the wrong person. Well, friends, God doesn't make mistakes. When He taps you for a job, He knows exactly what He's doing. He certainly did in the case of Moses, who also told God He had the wrong man for the job.

It is important to keep in mind that God generally does not call the *equipped* to fight His battles or become His witnesses. Rather, He *equips* those He calls with the tools they need to be successful. That process always involves being dependent on Him alone for courage and strength. In this sense, God is not necessarily looking for warriors. God is looking for people of valor—like you.

CHAPTER 16

Separation and Restoration

Now that you know you don't have to be Gideon or David or Moses to be a strong and effective witness for God, we can move to the exclamation point of this book—that is, what it looks like to tell people about God. That's what basic evangelism is all about: simply telling people what God has done for you.

At a deeper level, it's about explaining the biblical concepts of separation and restoration. Separation from God occurs as a result of sin. Restoration to the family of God occurs when sin is forgiven. Without restoration in this life, there's no promise of everlasting life with God in His spiritual kingdom. That constitutes spiritual death, and it leads to separation from God *for all eternity*.

Spiritual death is a very real risk because God is holy and without sin, whereas man is not holy and is by nature sinful. Sin entered the world because of Adam's and Eve's rebellion against God's instructions—His will. The idea of spiritual death and separation from God arose because of their sin. Adam and Eve were given a perfect place of sanctuary where all their needs were met. That sanctuary is known as the Garden of Eden (see Genesis 2:8).

The garden was planted with all kinds of trees, both pleasing to the eye and good for food. In the middle of the garden, God planted two specific trees. One was the tree of life, and the other was the tree of the knowledge of good and evil. Adam and Eve were free to eat of any tree in the garden, including from the tree of life. They were asked only to be obedient to

God's one wish—that they not eat the fruit of the tree of the knowledge of good and evil (see Genesis 2:9). God said that if Adam and Eve were to eat the fruit of that tree, they would surely die (see Genesis 2:17).

Consider this picture for a moment: A tree was placed in the middle of the garden and was clearly pointed out to Adam and Eve. They were told not to eat from it. But God put no fence or barrier around the tree. There was no moat around it filled with alligators. Ultimately, they were free to make their own choice whether to eat the fruit or not.

As it turned out, Eve was seduced by a serpent into eating that fruit on the promise that if she did, she would not die at all. Rather, if she ate the fruit, she would become like God (see Genesis 3:4). So Eve ate the fruit and gave some to Adam, and he also ate (see Genesis 3:6). God quickly discovered their sin—which was disobedience—and banished Adam and Eve from the garden (see Genesis 3:23).

The sin of Adam and Eve—original sin—caused the separation between man and God. Though it is true that Adam and Even didn't physically die of their sin (disobedience) that very day, they were in fact separated from God—both physically (as they were tossed out of the garden) and spiritually (they were no longer without sin).

We are all like Adam. At one level or another, to a greater or lesser extent, we have all sinned (see Romans 3:23). We are all separated from God. And without atonement for sin, mankind remains separated from God.

That separation means that we have lost God's overarching protection, not just in this earthly realm but for all eternity. For if we do not reconcile with God at some point during our lifetime, we die in that sin (see John 8:24). It's not like God sends lightning bolts to smite us, or puts pain, failure, and heartache directly in our paths expressly to punish us for such sin. But when we are out from under God's protective cover, we are at the mercy of a fallen and evil world—where anything can (and often does) happen.

There is no better explanation of this than the story Jesus tells of the lost son (often referred to as the prodigal son) in Luke 15. In the story

he father is the literary figure for God, and the son is the figure for humanity. The father was a wealthy man who owned land, raised crops and
livestock, had food to eat in abundance, and had many servants (see Luke
5:17). The son lived comfortably on his father's estate, under his care and
protection.

At some point, the son confronted his father, asking for his inheri-
ance. Under the Law of Moses, a son would get his father's estate only
upon the father's death (see Deuteronomy 21:17). However, a father could
decide to divide his estate earlier if he wished. Since the father made no
independent decision to divide the estate, and because the son demanded
his share while his father was yet alive, the son was essentially telling his
father, "You no longer matter to me. I don't need you. I'm going to leave
our household. You are dead to me."

Imagine the heartbreak and disappointment of a loving father who is
told this by his son. Imagine the confusion and frustration as the father
might try to reason with the boy to make him understand that everything
the father has belongs to the son, and that the father's oversight, care and
physical assets are all for the boy's protection, joy and prosperity. Yet the
boy would have none of it. Eventually the father shrugged his shoulders
and gave his defiant son his share of the estate, and then let him go (see
Luke 15:12).

With his money in hand, the boy took everything he had and traveled
to a distant land. We don't know where he went but that's not the point.
The message is clear that he left the protection of his father's estate and
oversight. It was the boy's voluntary choice. He was free to stay under his
father's protection but chose instead to leave, thus *himself* creating the
separation. It was his decision to go, just like it was Adam and Eve's decision to eat from the tree of the knowledge of good and evil. From that
point on, the son was on his own.

While he was off in some distant land, he didn't set up his own home
or use the money to fund a business or build a family. Instead, the boy

squandered all of his wealth in wild living (see Luke 15:13). He used it to pursue and satisfy his own hedonism. He rejected his father's physical protection, and he rejected his father's teachings of righteousness and sinless living. Just like Adam and Eve, the son rejected obedience to his father's way of life in favor of pursuing and satisfying his own base desires.

As you can imagine, with such a lifestyle it didn't take long for the kid to blow through the money. Eventually, it ran out (see Luke 15:14). In time, a famine came over the land. The boy had no means to provide for himself. He grew desperate and hungry to the point of hiring himself out to a local farmer to feed pigs (see Luke 15:15). Even at that, he was so hungry that he wished he could eat the food the pigs were eating—but he had nothing (see Luke 15:16).

Eventually, the boy came to his senses (see Luke 15:17). He said to himself that even his father's servants had food to spare but here he was starving to death. He clearly recognized the folly of his initial rebellious and immature choices. He made the decision to return to his father's estate and the protection his father offered (see Luke 15:18). Under his father's protection, he had it all—not just land, food and physical protection, but also the covering of his father's love and graciousness.

Imagine if the boy had died while separated from this father. His relationship would not have been restored. By dying in his sin, he would have been separated from that love and gracious covering for all eternity. While we are yet alive in the physical sense, there exists the capacity to restore our relationship with God the Father in the spiritual sense. We can recognize our own rebelliousness and immaturity in rejecting God or, as in many cases, our ignorance of God's gracious love and His desire to provide that protective covering for all of us.

Adam and Eve's situation in the garden was no different. The tree of life represents the love and grace of God and His protection and care. Eat from the tree of life and you enjoy community with God and life everlasting. The tree of the knowledge of good and evil represents the hedonistic self-centered, base desires of mankind: sinfulness and disobedience. Eat of that tree and you become separated from God. You quickly learn, just as the rebellious kid in Luke 15 learned, that the world is an evil, ugly, cold and heartless place. Through his separation from his father, the kid indeed learned the hard way about the difference between good and evil. He witnessed and lived through evil, danger, hunger and hopelessness. He learned that what he had under his father's protection was much more desirable by any measure than the evil of the world.

The boy returned to his father before it was too late (see Luke 15:18). And this is where the story gets fascinating.

Upon the return of the lost son, the father does five remarkable things:

1. When he saw the kid coming, the father was filled with compassion. He ran off to meet his son. He put his arms around him and kissed him (see Luke 15:20). What message do you suppose this sent to the kid? It tells him, "You are loved. You belong here. You were missed and you were never forgotten." As the son comes face-to-face with his father, you can imagine the shame, embarrassment and guilt he must have felt. But while he was in the very act of apologizing, his father interrupted him. He interrupted to tell his servants to bring his son the best robe, to put sandals on his feet, and to put a ring on his finger (see Luke 15:22-23).

2. Yes, the second thing the father did was to order that the best robe be brought for the son. There can be little doubt that the son's clothes were tattered and filthy. The act of clothing the son with the best robe is a symbol that the father took away the son's guilt. Zechariah describes this very thing in his vision of Joshua standing before God's angel. Joshua was wearing filthy clothes, a symbol of sin. The angel tells his attendants to remove Joshua's filthy clothes and to put "fine garments" on him (see Zechariah 3:4-5). By removing the filthy clothes and giving him the finest robe, the son's sins were cleansed at that moment. He was made pure and without sin.

3. The third thing the father did was to have sandals put on his son's feet. This is significant and has nothing to do with the boy's posture. In the first century, only slaves went barefoot. Freemen wore shoes. This is powerful symbolism to illustrate that the kid was no longer a slave to sin and death. The kid was set free of that bondage and, with that, he was set free of his shame, embarrassment and guilt.

4. The fourth thing the father did was to put a ring on his son's finger. I promise you, the ring wasn't given to adorn the kid with bling. The ring is also an important symbol. It signifies full restoration to the family. The ring is a symbol that the son has the authority to act for his father. This is exactly what Pharaoh did when he made Joseph second in command over all of Egypt. We read in Genesis 41:39-43 that upon ordaining Joseph, Pharaoh gave Joseph his signet ring. The ring was proof that Joseph had full authority to act on Pharaoh's behalf. The act of putting the ring on the kid's finger symbolizes his full and perfect restoration to the family. It once again entitles the son to a full inheritance of his father's estate, despite the fact that he squandered it once already.

5. The last thing the father did was to call for the fatted calf. He ordered that it be killed and made ready for a feast. He ordered that there was to be a celebration. Why? Verse 24 explains why: The father says that "this son of mine was dead and is alive again; he was lost and is found."

Now the most incredible part of this story, and the part we must focus on in our witness to the lost, is what the father did *not* do. He put no conditions on any of this. He didn't demand a public apology. He didn't put the kid on family probation to see how he might act going forward. He didn't require restitution for the money his son blew in wild living. Instead, the son's return to his father, his admission that he sinned (see Luke 15:18), and his request for forgiveness (see Luke 15:19,21) led to full, absolute restoration and unconditional forgiveness. That was driven solely by the father's unfailing love for his son that never stopped, despite what his son did.

Each of us is just like that kid in some way. We are unappreciative, selfish, greedy, hedonistic, or reckless. We believe our way is better than God's way. We reject His loving care and guidance. We willingly walk into an evil and fallen world without God's overarching protection and are somehow surprised when things go terribly wrong. But just like the prodigal son, we can experience this same glorious, unconditional love, forgiveness and restoration to God's family.

You might ask your unsaved friends these questions:

- Do you want to feel the kiss of reconciliation from God Himself?
- Do you want to be wiped clean of all your guilt, shame and embarrassment?
- Do you want to be adorned with a robe of righteousness?
- Do you want to wear the sandals of freedom?
- Do you want to wear a ring bearing the signet of almighty God?
- Do you want to be the guest of honor at a banquet in God's kingdom?

All these things can be yours if you just return to the feet of the father, just like the prodigal son did in Luke 15, confess that you are a sinner, and ask forgiveness in the name of Jesus Christ. At that moment, you will be restored.

Do not make the mistake of believing that your sin is too great, your failures are too profound, or your shame is too deep to warrant God's forgiveness and restoration. In Romans, Paul makes it perfectly clear that we all have sinned; we all have fallen short of God's standard of perfect holiness (see Romans 3:23; 3:10). We are all just like the prodigal son, to one degree or another. And yet, the father never forgot his son and never stopped loving him. It bears restating (as I said in chapter 13) that as the son was making his way home in his shame and guilt, no doubt dreading the idea of facing his father, his father saw him while he was still a long way off. He saw the boy coming from a great distance *because he was looking for him* (see Luke 15:20)!

He's looking for you too, and He will welcome you home with the same great joy and celebration as He did the prodigal.

ABOUT THE AUTHOR

Dan Pilla's primary calling is that of tax litigator. He is considered America's leader in taxpayers' rights defense and IRS abuse prevention and cure. Regarded as one of the country's premiere experts in IRS procedures and general financial-problems resolution techniques, he has helped hundreds of thousands of citizens solve personal and business tax and financial problems they thought might never be solved.

As the author of fifteen books, dozens of research reports, and well over a thousand articles, Dan's work is regularly featured on radio and television, as well as in major newspapers, leading magazines and trade publications nationwide. Dan is a frequent guest on numerous talk radio and TV programs where he is heard by millions of people each year.

Dan works with various local and national Christian organizations, teaching God's Word in churches across America. Topics relate to tax and financial issues as well as life's general challenges.

Dan served on the board of directors of various Christian organizations over the years. He currently works closely, as a board member and a ministry team member, with a local church and a Christian men's group. In that role, he developed the curriculum for a men's Bible study group which he has taught for the past four years.

He lives and works in Stillwater, Minnesota (east of St. Paul), with his wife, Jean, of 32 years, and their family.

OTHER WRITINGS
BY DAN PILLA

What is America's DNA?

How to Win Your Tax

How to Get Tax Amnesty

The IRS Problem Solver

How to Eliminate Taxes on Debt Forgiveness

How to Double Your Tax Refund

Taxpayers' Ultimate Defense Manual

Ten Principals of Federal Tax Policy

1-800-346-6829

www.taxhelponline.com

WINNING Publications, Inc.

215 W. Myrtle Street

Stillwater, MN 55082